From Turmoil to Triumph

Dave Sanderson

Turmoil to Triumph

ISBN 978-0-578-26021-1

Table of Contents

Dedication

From Turmoil to Triumph is dedicated to my mother and father, Erma and Keith Sanderson. You gave me life and so much more. You were the first to teach me important lessons that would not only help me through life but also helped save my life on January 15, 2009. I love you more than I ever told you when you were alive.

This book is also dedicated to my first mentor, Bill. If my father hadn't followed through on his edict that I had thirty days to move out of my childhood home after I graduated from James Madison University, I would have probably never met you. We spent many lunches and dinners talking about things that would help me become the man I am today.

You would not have believed that those lessons initially received as lessons for success would coalesce on one fateful day in January 2009 and help me live my dream. Those lessons didn't die with you, and I won't let them die with me. I will find someone who will pass them on so they can have the fulfillment and happiness I have had, and the lessons will live on.

My Mom and Dad

Foreword

As an entrepreneur with years of experience working with a variety of leaders in many different industries, I am always looking for why people achieve the results they do. There are some people who become successful, while others struggle to achieve even the slightest success. Still others just seem lucky—but since I believe that "Luck favors the prepared," it was only natural to begin a search for the secrets to success. What is the why? The results came after my five-year doctoral study of the elite performers in the world—business and personal—and what made them who they are. Thus, my book, *The Perfect Plan*.

One day, I was listening to a lecture in Chicago, and the speaker was telling a story about his new friend, Dave Sanderson, and his experience of surviving a plane crash. "Wow!" I thought. Surviving a plane crash is an amazing experience on its own, but what hooked me was how the speaker explained the effect it had on Dave's life and his commitment to serving others.

After a bit of research and a few phone calls, I was thrilled to be speaking voice-to-voice with Dave, and that's when he touched my life and changed it for the better.

I learned that Dave was in sales and was a top producer. That was no surprise, but I also learned that Dave possessed the same traits as the world's elite performers I had just finished studying. To be frank, I am always looking to see if the hypothesis I wrote about is accurate, and Dave easily fit into the analysis. The concept is simple: is there a secret sauce that separates the world's 99 percent from the top 1 percent? When I met Dave Sanderson, I knew he had the extra thing that made him one of the elites, and for years he has proven it over and over again.

I was honored when Dave accepted our invitation to speak at a client event in Atlanta, Georgia. After I heard his presentation and saw the response from the attendees, I knew there was something special about Dave and his message to the world. He and I struck up a relationship, and I invited him to participate withDominique Wilkins, Steve Nedvidek, and Brittany Tucker to work with small businesses and teach servant leadership to the world's aspiring leaders.

A year after we met, Dave called me and shared something he found. While writing his book, *Moments Matter*, Dave discovered a series of older notes from his first mentor. He told me how important these notes were to him and, more importantly, the promise he made to himself to share them with the world. I toldDave, "I believe God gives you the lesson when you are ready, and now is the time to share them with the world."

I am proud to say that Dave has been working for five years to bring these lessons to the world. Dave understands the value of having mentors in his life, and I've been honoured that he looks to me for friendship and guidance.

In 2016, Dave was asked to do a TEDx Talk that was close to his heart. He named it "Bouncing Back: An Experience with Post-Traumatic Growth Syndrome." Dave has a passion for helping those who have gone through a harrowing life experience, but I dare say, he did not know how prophetic that topic would become. As we all come to realize the new reality of the post-pandemic world, Dave is needed now more than ever.

When COVID-19 hit in 2020, the world was changed. Dave took that time to reach out to people worldwide to find out what they were experiencing and how he could help. He soon discovered that 2020 was not only about COVID-19; it was about the social justice questions, police issues, and a never-ending election that split up friends and family. It was about turmoil.

Dave and I discussed on several occasions the need to adapt and adjust with people's lives. Dave knew the time was right to teach and share the lessons of his mentors, and to help people turn their personal turmoil into a victory—better yet, a triumph.

When Dave asked me to pen the foreword for this enlightening, entertaining, and often touching book, there was no question what my answer would be. In basketball parlance, this was an uncontested slam-dunk.

I say this not because of Dave's many professional accomplishments, nor how Dave has been recognized for what he has done in his sales career, but, more importantly, how he has given his time, talents, and money back to organizations such as the American Red Cross and veteran causes. In the past decade, he has helped raise over $14 million to help others in need.

Wow!

Dave knows what it means to be a true friend. He understands that loyalty is a two-way street. He is an extraordinary "point of light" who generously supports anyone who may be going through a difficult time. Most of all, as you will soon discover, Dave is a devoted father, husband, and friend. Just spend about fifteen minutes around Dave, and you will know the deepest currents that shaped who he has become.

What you will discover in *From Turmoil to Triumph* are the timeless lessons of success. Each is presented in a way to help you reflecton the people who have come into your life and taught you things when you needed it the most—those special lessons, especially when you may have been at your lowest of lows.

One of the things that helped Dave when he faced turmoil in hislife was his realization that he could not do it alone. You need to have a wingman with you, a mentor who can bring out the lessons you need at just the right time.

So, what I realized during my time with Dave is that the biggest turmoil of his life, the infamous Miracle on the Hudson, on January 15, 2009, became the test of all the lessons he had learned. Everything in his life seemed to lead up to that fateful date and the events that occurred in the Hudson River with overone hundred passengers on a failed flight. Dave, as only he cando, used those lessons to save lives, and he continues to this dayto be committed to serving everyone he meets.

Dave Sanderson is the real thing. He lives his life as an authentic servant leader, and in this book, he shares how he turned turmoil into triumph.

So, sit back and enjoy this remarkable personal journey that spans close to sixty years. Learn how you too can use these timeless lessons taught by a mentor who committed them to Dave, even when Dave didn't understand why. Learn how an eager young man would one day use these lessons to not only survive a plane crash, but also to help others turn their turmoil to triumph.

Don Barden

Author, Economist, and CEO

Prologue: You Choose Your Destiny

January 15, 2009

That day was the end of a whirlwind business trip that started Tuesday in Sarasota, Florida; then, on Wednesday I was at my client's manufacturing plant in Petersburg, Virginia. After that, I jumped on a train to New York City late that afternoon to finish up my week of travel in Brooklyn at their distribution center.

My day started at 5:00 a.m. Distribution centers open early in the morning. This one opened at 2:00 a.m., but I didn't get there quite that early. We finished at the distribution center earlier than I'd planned, and excited to get back home, I jumped on the phone to change my flight to Charlotte. I was scheduled to leave at 5:00 p.m., but I told them to put me on the earliest flight out from LaGuardia that I could get to. Our corporate travel agent put me on the afternoon flight, 1549, in seat 15A. I was happy to give up my first-class seat on the other flight so I could get home early and surprise my family.

I loved having chairman status with US Airways (the highest one), as it allowed me to board early. I went to my seat, pulled the magazine out, and started to read. I didn't pay attention to the flight attendant, as I had heard the speech many times before and could almost recite it by heart. Little did I know that choosing to board the earlier flight would change the course of my destiny.

My family probably gets tired of me saying, "You chose that option." I learned many years ago, first from my mother, then from other people in my life, that the path your life takes comes down to a choice. Many whom I speak with, including my family, often talk to me about things in their lives as if they have no control over the options. They say, "I have to do it." I, too, have said that many times in the past, but I have learned that the reason I am where I am today is because I chose a specific pathway.

Something came to light for me after I watched the movie *Dr. Strange*. In this film, the lead character says at one point, "I am not ready." The response from the Ancient One is, "No one ever is. We don't get to choose our time."

As happens many times in a busy airport, the flights were backed up. Our flight was delayed by traffic as well as the weather and temperature. Finally, we took off. About sixty seconds in, I heard an explosion and looked out the window. I saw fire coming out from underneath the left wing. That was ominous, but I knew we had another engine. I figured we would be going back to the airport to get another plane. So much for getting home early!

No one in the cabin knew at that moment that what happened on the left side of the aircraft had also happened on the right side, and the plane lost all power. When the plane banked left instead of right to go back to LaGuardia, I knew that something waswrong, but it wasn't until we started to cross over the George Washington Bridge and cleared it by about 400 feet that I knew it was a dire situation. That was the moment when all the investment in my personal development, lessons, and skills I learned throughout my life started to kick in. I quickly put together a game plan and focused on the execution.

The first thing I did was asked God to forgive my sins. I had faith that whatever happened, my family and I were going to be all right. I had to stay optimistic if I was going to have a chance to survive. As I tried to brace for impact, I saw the movie of my life clearly pass before my eyes, and at that moment I knew what my life was all about. I thought, "If I survive, I need to make decisions quickly. Execute, execute, execute." I had never seen a plane crash in the water successfully, and I knew the plane would probably have fire upon impact. It was also going to be a long shot at surviving after the crash in ice-cold water.

The impact was hard and violent. Once the plane stopped, I looked up and saw the light out my window, and I knew now was my chance. It was the time to execute the game plan I had put together seconds earlier: aisle, up, out.

Later, when I was interviewed by Katie Couric on the CBS Evening News, the term I used to describe the moment in the plane was controlled chaos, as people were composed but moving quickly. Staying composed was extremely important. I knew that if I started to get emotional, others might get that way also, and all of us might lose focus.

I looked up and saw people climbing over the seats and realized there was more than one way to get out of the plane. When I got to the aisle, I had accomplished part one of my plan. Now it was time for up and out.

At that moment, I heard my mother's voice in my head. She said, "If you do the right thing, God will take care of you." A gift my mother and father gave me was the ability to make decisions for myself and be accountable for them. I knew what I had to do.

I climbed over the seats toward the back of the plane to see if anyone needed help, rather than going forward for my own exit. Fortunately, people were moving, and I got behind the last person to make sure there was nobody left behind. I worked my way up to the first light I saw on the right side of the plane at seat 10F and started to make my way out. As I looked out, I noticed that the wing was already filled up with passengers, the rescue boat was filled with passengers, and people were already being taken to safety.

I heard people yelling at me to hold onto the plane because the lifeboat was floating out into the fast current of the ice-cold Hudson River, and I had the leverage to grasp the plane's door. I decided to take responsibility for holding onto the plane. For seven minutes, I held the packed lifeboat next to the plane's exit door so people could get off the lifeboat and onto the wing to make their way to the ferries.

About seven minutes later, I felt the plane shift and thought it was going down. "This is it," I thought. "I have to go or be pulled down to the bottom of the river." I had to take massive action and employ a skill I learned when I was young: swimming. Thank God my mother had pushed me to get my junior lifeguard certification! I jumped in and swam the length of the wing, the longest fifteen-yard swim of my life. I got to the ferry, but now had to get on it. I yelled, "I can't!" but when I said that, I thought of my mom again. She would *never* let us say that word. I got one arm up, then the other, and two men pulled me up. Massive teamwork helped me get onto the ferry.

Through perseverance, I survived the crash; now I had to survive the cold, as it was 11°F (-23°C). I was blessed that now the extended rescue team could take over and help me. I was taken to the ferry station in Weehawken, New Jersey.

When the EMTs and Red Cross volunteer put me on the floor, the EMTs ripped my clothes off down to my underwear. I looked to my left, and the gentleman next to me was also in his underwear. I looked to my right and saw a young lady with nothing on. I quickly realized the magnitude of what was going on and was overwhelmed with humility.

A few minutes later, after my vitals were taken, I was rushed to Palisades Medical Center, where a group of nurses carried me to a bed. Waiting was a doctor and other nurses to take care of me. One of the first things the nurses did was take my temperature, first orally, then anally, and they stripped me down to nothing! My temperature was 94°F (34.4°C) and dropping quickly, and I was diagnosed with hypothermia.

As the nurses and doctor were working on me, the hospital chaplain came over and asked me if I was okay and if I wanted to pray. I told him I did, and he brought a copy of the New Testament, placed it on my chest, and we prayed. Faith helped me survive and is now helping me recover.

I have thought many times about the events of that day and how my life changed, and I am incredibly humbled. I was very fortunate to have people in my life who gave me the lessons and knowledge I needed to make the right choices throughout that day. *I did not choose my time.* I wasn't supposed to be on that plane that day. I believe it was a defining moment, the test of everything that I had learned and prepared for throughout my life.

When I think about that day, I am reminded of the story of Jacob in the Old Testament. Jacob was returning home to his family as he fled his brother Esau. He got to the river, and his family crossed, but he didn't. Throughout the night, he wrestled with someone. Most scholars think it was God in a human form, and that Jacob wrestled with the Divine.

In the *Morfix – English toHebrew Translator & Dictionary*, one definition for wrestling means "engaged." Jacob wasn't boxing with God; he was wrestling and fully engaged throughout the night with God.

During the struggle, God struck Jacob's hip and injured it, but Jacob never let go. At daybreak, God in human form said, "Let me go," but Jacob would not until he was blessed. God then blessed Jacob and changed his name to Israel. Jacob's identity was changed at that moment. He called the place where he struggled face-to-face with God, *Peniel,* and his life was spared. Jacob limped away, scarred but alive, with a new identity, and a new mission.

I was asked a few years ago to speak at the 9/11 service in UnionCounty, North Carolina. My minister, Ken Carter, had never heard me speak outside the church, so I invited him and my assistant, Tammy, to go with me. We went to Monroe, NC that morning, along with other dignitaries, law enforcement, and military officials. I keynoted the event.

When we were walking back to the car, Reverend Carter said something that may have summed up what happened on January 15, 2009. He said, "In the Christian faith, we are baptized into the faith once, but when I heard you today,I thought about the moment you jumped in the water and had faith, and when you came out you were a different person with a new mission. It was like you were baptized again." Maybe coming out of the water that day, I was "baptized again" with a new direction for my life, a new course, and an opportunity to fulfill what I had committed to Bill in 1997, to "not let it die with me."

What I do know is this: all the moments in our lives matter. That moment on January 15, 2009, was life-changing for me, but there were many other moments that changed the direction of my life, little by little, over time. You never know when someone will come into your life, and who will share with you something that may save your life and change your future. As Jesus told His disciples that fateful night in the Garden, "Stay awake." We always need to be ready and open to accept these lessons that our mentors are giving us.

Putting It into Practice

Choice is an enormous power that we have, and there are two things we have to know to unleash that massive power. First, as Tony Robbins teaches, our destiny is shaped not by the circumstances that come our way, but by the choices we make. Second, we must use power to act on the choices we make. If we want to improve our lives, we must improve the choices we make. The sooner we recognize that every decision has consequences, the better we will become at thinking ahead. Acting impulsively might be fine in choosing what to have for dinner, but it can be disastrous as a strategy when your life is on the line. We are not God.

As US Airways Flight 1549 made its final descent into the Hudson River, I thought it might be the last moments of my life. I was wrestling with all the things I was never going to be able to do, and all the people in my life that I was never going to see again. When I started to employ all that I learned throughout my life to survive, things began to coalesce. When I got to the aisle and heard my mother's voice in my head, I realized that my choices in life had prepared me for this moment.

My mother was in heaven with God, and I believe she was sitting at His left hand with Him next to her when she was speaking to me. I believe that she and Bill had interacted in heaven before this day and discussed the lessons they both gave me. Now it was time for The Test. All the things that she and Bill taught me and that I learned throughout my life were coming to play. Just like God wrestled with Jacob, my mother was testing me, making sure I was fully engaged.

Years ago, when we lost our son, Thomas, Bill had said, "The same God that brought you into life is the same one that is with your son now." The same God that was at the beginning was with Jesus on the cross—and was with my mother and Bill in heaven—and is the same one who was with me that day. Some scholars say that it wasn't God who wrestled with Jacob, but a man that God inhabited. I don't know, but the more I think about it, the more I wonder if, throughout my life and all our lives, God represents Himself through the people who come into our lives to teach usthe lessons we need to be the person we are meant to be.

Maybe God was in my mother at those moments as she was giving me those lessons. Maybe God was in Bill when he took me on for thirteen years and taught me what he learned and what I needed to learn. Maybe God was in Bill's mentor when he was teaching Bill.

I thought about that and thought of Jacob. Perhaps January 15, 2009, was The Test for me. I didn't let go. I didn't give up. I employed all the lessons I had learned to survive that day. Because I made the right choices and did the right thing, my lifewas about to change. That test put me on a new course just like it did for Jacob.

God gave me the lesson and now I am ready. Are you?

It's rare to have two of my mentors with me at the same time. I invited them to go to something we all love: a Major League Baseball game at SunTrust Park between the Atlanta Braves and my favorite team, the Cincinnati Reds!

Introduction

Sometimes, all it takes is a single moment to change the course of your entire life.

The fall of 1977 was one of those times. I was riding high, excelling on the varsity football team, getting ready for a big year on the varsity basketball team, and doing well in the classroom. I was the starting center on the varsity football team. During a game against Woodbridge, I was going for a stretch block, and someone hit me right on the knee. As a result, I suffered a season-ending injury—a torn knee ligament. I had never felt pain like that before, and I was about to face something I had never faced before.

I was devastated.

I started rehab, but in my teenage mindset I felt like my life was over—until David, who was with the Kiwanis Club, came into my life and asked me to help him begin a new Key Club at the high school. David mentored me on how to be a leader, how to step up and take responsibility, and how to begin something new from scratch. That experience was life-changing for me, as not only did we start a new club that would have over a hundred people involved in the next year, but also, he introduced me to people I would have never met had I had not been injured.

One of those people was Harry Byrd, Jr., our U.S. Senator for my home state of Virginia. Through that introduction, I was invited to attend an event where one of my childhood heroes, senator and astronaut John Glenn, spoke. David introduced me to world leaders, to how they think, and how they can influence society. He taught me to stay aware and be open to the possibilities that life would offer me. He and I could have never envisioned where that would lead.

In the short term, my new outlook led me to college at James Madison University. I graduated in 1983 into an economy coming out of recession. Jobs were hard to get, especially in international business, which was the discipline I chose. Like many of my parents' generation, moving home after college wasn't an option for me. My dad told me I had thirty days to find a job after graduation, and at the end of that time I would be out of the house.

One thing my dad taught me is that your word is your bond, and he stuck to that with me. At the end of the thirty days, I still didn't have a job. My dad helped me get one as a second assistant restaurant manager at Howard Johnson. I was out of the house with a job I knew nothing about, but like that fateful night at the football game, this move would changemy destiny.

Eventually, my Howard Johnson's job took me to Charlotte, North Carolina. I was put on second shift with Jim Moran, my general manager. He was a great business mentor and taught me all about hotel and restaurant management. I loved working for him, but it was one of the customers I met on that shift who would change the course of my life.

Every night, a couple came into the restaurant for coffee and ice cream. Bill and his wife, Bonnie, drove a pickup truck, and Bill always wore a flannel shirt. I got to know them as regulars, andwe had great discussions. One evening during one of those discussions, he gave me a pass to a movie theater to take a girlout for a date. All he asked of me was to tell him about my experience at the theater. I soon found out that he owned that theater and wanted me to share with him what I thought.

When I came back to give him my review, I discovered that he owned many movie theaters in North and South Carolina. He was known locally as the Sam Walton of Charlotte. He and I continued our evening discussions, and then one fateful day he changed up our routine and came in during the afternoon instead.

"Come check out the Christmas present I got for Bonnie," Bill said.

I went outside to see a brand-new shiny blue Corvette. I'd never seen a Corvette, let alone a new one.

"Let's go for a spin," he said, and threw me the keys. It was exhilarating.

"You need to get one of those," Bill said, jokingly. At that time,I was only making about $13,000 a year. I could barely afford rent, let alone a payment on a sports car.

"I could never afford something like that," I said.

"That's your problem, son," he said. "You need to change your mindset."

At that point, Bill offered to mentor me, and I accepted. For the next thirteen years, during good times and bad, he taught me the mindset for success and personal leadership.

Bill taught me through the stories of how he got where he was in life. He shared the lessons, disciplines, and habits that I could apply immediately for greater success in my own life.

In 1997, Bill called me to come to his house for a talk. I thought it would be like any other visit, but when I arrived, he told me he had lung cancer. As we talked, he walked over to his desk, pulled out a stack of papers, and came over to sit next to me. He told me the papers had the handwritten notes he took in 1929 from his mentor, George, who taught him the principles of business success. These were the lessons he was giving me over those thirteen years.

That day, Bill gave the papers to me, making me promise I wouldn't let the lessons die with me. In September 1997, that same year, Bill passed away. He died without ever knowing the impact he had on me and my life.

Over the past twenty-plus years, those lessons imparted by Bill have lived within me and shaped my life, but it wasn't until I ran across the handwritten notes a few years back that I remembered the promise I had made. I had to find a way to pass on Bill's knowledge, to not let it die with me.

This book is a compilation of the stories I heard over those years with Bill. These pages contain the lessons, strategies, and habits that helped him become a tremendous business leader and one of the wealthiest and most successful people I have ever met. More than that, he had one thing that many, if not most,successful and wealthy individuals don't have. In addition to financial success, he lived a life of personal happiness and fulfillment. He was able to take the turmoil he encountered throughout his life and turn it into a triumph for himself, but more importantly, for the people he encountered. He was a servant leader: the essence of true success.

In the pages that follow, you will learn the twelve principles that Bill first discovered in 1929, which he then passed on to me during our friendship from 1984 to 1997. Each one on its own merit can help you make significant progress in your personal and business life. Taken together, all twelve principles coalesce, and you will move toward being fulfilled. That is what I call the Point In Time That Changes Everything—your PITTChE. It's when you understand what your mission is, you are passionate about it, and that you will be fulfilled. Following these principles will help you achieve success on your terms and a life of happiness.

That moment came to me on January 15, 2009. That day, I survived the plane crash known as the Miracle on the Hudson.

That's when I learned that moments do matter. All those strategies I had learned came together in that one moment to help me find my inner strength and survive one of the most terrifying days of my life. I was equipped to start turning the turmoil from that fateful time into a triumph—

first in my own life, but as it turned out, also in the lives of many others whom I have encountered along the way.

I learned that day that you will never know which one moment will change the course of your life, but when that moment comes, you must be prepared. Through my time with Bill, learning his strategies and disciplines, I was ready. You can be, too. No single lesson will carry you to the pinnacle, but taken together, these lessons can change your date with destiny.

Lesson One:
Demand More of Yourself

October 24, 1929

The world changed for the worse for many people when the stock market crashed, leading to the Great Depression. But for a young twenty-three-year-old man from small-town North Carolina, that day marked the beginning of a bright, successful future.

This young man loved moving pictures. He was mesmerized by their ability to tell stories. He dreamed of having his own place where he could show these movies to other people, but he had a problem—he didn't have any money. He couldn't afford to buy a place to show movies, let alone rent the movies to show.

On that fateful day in October, this young man traveled with his dad to Charlotte, North Carolina, to take the crops to market. During that trip, he and his dad were eating lunch in a restaurant when they struck up a conversation with a businessman in Charlotte. The young man talked about his dream of having a moving picture theater. The businessman took an interest in the young man, and they kept in touch.

A few months later, they reconnected.

"I know a way to get your dream of a movie theater up and running," the businessman said.

"But isn't it too risky?"

The young man saw the long lines of unemployed people waiting just to get bread and wasn't sure if this was the right time for investments. But the older gentleman reassured him, and with his advice and guidance, the young man built his first moving picture theater.

Over the next fifty-plus years, that one theater grew to many more and he became a wealthy man, not only financially but also spiritually and emotionally. That young man, Bill, became my mentor, passing on to another generation the keys to success in life.

Bill and I met in 1983, when I was working second shift at the Howard Johnson's. He and his wife came in every night for coffee, and those conversations we had were the start of a long friendship and mentor relationship. In 1986, my job took me from Charlotte to Vienna, Virginia.

I left my fiancée back in Charlotte and moved, hoping to further my career. We kept the relationship going, even though the long distance had its challenges, and I continued to talk with Bill as well. His advice was critical to me as I learned the ropes of management.

In December 1986, I had a big decision to make. The Marriott Corporation purchased Howard Johnson's, which opened a new track for me in hotel and restaurant management. It also meant that if I was going to be a general manager of my own restaurant, I had to be open to moving.

The track to general manager went north, not south. Just a few days before Christmas, in one of our busiest times, my general manager came to me and told me it was time for me to be a general manager. He told me I'd be going to either Baltimore, Maryland, or Philadelphia, Pennsylvania.

Of course, the first person I talked with about that offer was my fiancée. Terri told me she wasn't moving north, so I had to make a decision: take the promotion and possibly give up on my relationship, or give up my promotion, start over, and marry Terri. I called Bill. His advice changed the course of my life.

He told me I could always get a job, but I may never find anyone like Terri again. He had taught me through his relationship with his own wife that putting relationships first is a key to happiness. Now it was time to figure out my own priorities in life. I gave up my promotion and moved back to Charlotte to be with Terri.

Bill's advice was right on point, as I quickly got a job as a restaurant manager at Shoney's. Over the next year, I worked my way up that chain, getting promoted to one of their top stores in Monroe, North Carolina, just a short drive from Charlotte. Things were going well—or so I thought.

In May 1987, I was asked to be in my sister's wedding in Winchester, Virginia. I needed an entire weekend off to be part of the wedding party, but Shoney's policy was that managers could only have one day off. When I was with Marriott, managers had two days off every week and there was excellent employee morale, so I knew it could work at Shoney's. I had already implemented some policies from Marriott into the operation at Shoney's, and this seemed like a logical next step. I arranged to have my first assistant manager run the store for the weekend. That weekend was the beginning of the summer season, and the store was right on the way to Myrtle Beach, South Carolina. We were very busy, but everything ran fine.

When I got back in town, I was called to meet with my regional manager. I expected to be praised for implementing a new policy that worked so well. Instead, he told me that was not the way Shoney's system was run. He and I agreed that I needed to find another place to work.

Again, I called Bill. Here I was, a newlywed, and out of a job again.

Bill said, "That's great news!"

"What?" I was dumbfounded.

He said this was the opportunity I needed to grow. It was time for me to find a job that not only gave me joy, but also helped me make more money. I didn't realize it at first, but Bill was giving me the first lesson to success: demand more of yourself.

This time, when I started interviewing for jobs, I broadened my horizons, looking outside the restaurant management career path. I ended up with a job as a copier salesman. I knew nothing about selling or copiers, but I saw it as a way to learn something new. I had a great trainer, Matt, and I quickly grasped the concepts of selling.

Matt took particular interest in me, training me in the copier products and the basics of selling, including handling rejection. I learned so fast that I won the local and regional Demo-Rama contest, a contest that tests salesmen on their knowledge and competency to present a high-level copier. I went on to get second place in the national Demo-Rama.

Things were going well until a new manager came into the office. He had a different mentality than Matt. He was more focused on moving products than growing people. Bill and I talked about the managers' different styles, and he said it might be time for me to look for another job.

"If you're working for someone who is driven only by the bottom line, you'll never be given the opportunity to grow," Bill said. "One thing I learned as a manager and business owner is that the key to overall success is giving people room to learn and grow."

Bill was correct. A couple of months later, that manager and I had a disagreement. I knew it was time to go, and fortunately, I already had another job lined up.

I was excited to start training at this new job, but I found out that what most companies call sales training is really product training. Bill told me that if I was really going to grow to my full potential, I needed to invest in my own training outside the company. It was time for me to start developing not only my sales skills, but also my mindset, my physical self, and my philosophy.

Bill told me a story about when he started working with his mentor. As a child, Bill had only gone to school through the sixth grade. That year, World War I broke out, and Bill had to spend more time working on the farm with his father to raise the crops. He eventually finished high school but then went back to the farm. He wasn't a big reader; he learned by watching his father and others.

Once Bill started working with his mentor, he insisted that Bill begin reading to develop his mind, as it would give him more resources to make decisions. His advice to Bill was, "To have more than you've got, become more than you are." Bill's mentor taught him not to be satisfied with just meeting other people's expectations for him. He needed to demand more of himself.

Bill started to read. He devoured the classics, like *The Great Gatsby*, *Main Street*, and *The Great Impersonation*. He began to learn things from other people that he could apply to his business and personal life, and he started growing his mind and business.

Bill shared what he learned from books with his mentor, and his mentor supplemented it with his own experiences. That one nugget of wisdom from his mentor, to demand more of himself, helped Bill understand the importance of owning one's own development. Bill was now encouraging me to do the same.

I started reading too, books like *Think and Grow Rich*. I was learning things, but I wanted to get on the fast track. I was 26 and wanted to make my move. That's when Bill introduced me to a new form of personal development, beyond books. He asked if I'd ever gone to a seminar, and he suggested that I check out this guy named Tom Hopkins.

I went to my vice president of sales, Gordon Lane, and asked him about the Tom Hopkins seminar. He told me the company wouldn't pay for it, but he would give me the time off to go if I wanted to. I signed up to go.

After that first seminar in 1988, I started to invest more into my own personal development. Every year, I went to at least one seminar where I was exposed to different ways of thinking. I learned from great people like Tom Hopkins, Jim Rohn, Dennis Waitley, and Tony Robbins. I shared what I learned with Bill, and we discussed the ideas and how I could apply them to my life and business.

Since Bill started me on my personal development journey, a significant portion of my life is spent getting ready and preparing. Tony Robbins calls it CANI: Constant And Never-ending Improvement. Every outstanding leader starts with personal development, practicing it every day to make measurable progress.

Putting It into Practice

As you know, January 15, 2009, was a day that changed my life forever. I'm often asked what saved my life that day. Of course, I attribute everyone's survival to the teamwork of the crew, the passengers, and the first responders. It was amazing how everybody checked their egos and focused on pulling together to help each other.

Without having to speak the words, we were all on the same page and had the same mission. We had an unspoken vow to help each other survive. In addition to that amazing teamwork, I truly believe that for me, all those moments of preparation, all the time spent investing in my personal development mentally, emotionally, spiritually, and physically was a determining factor in my survival.

Personal development is a struggle. It's challenging, but I have learned that you cannot grow without change. That's what life is all about. It's a struggle and a challenge to develop our skills, to see how we can create even more value in the marketplace; in our finances; in our physical, mental, and spiritual health; and in our relationships.

It all starts with building momentum in one direction. Bill liked to say that success is 10 percent inspiration and 90 percent perspiration. It's a lot of work to read the books, learn the skills, put yourself through the paces, do the mental push-ups, and get yourself ready, but that hard work always pays off. Bill's encouragement to demand more of myself has served me well many times in my life. Especially during the Miracle on the Hudson.

Make Personal Growth Your New Mindset

Bill pushed me to read more and explore new options for personal growth, but that wasn't the first time I had heard that message. Like many children, I was exposed to those habits in athletics and Scouting. I knew that if I wanted to make the team or if I wanted to be an Eagle Scout, I had to push myself to practice and to learn.

I had to do more than what was required; I had to reach further to really stand out. Later, as an adult, I took those practices and applied them to push myself further in my professional skill sets. My parents had taught me to have a good work ethic, and Bill took it a step further by teaching me the importance of investing in myself and my personal development and putting what I had learned into action.

There have been times when I have not acted upon what I have learned, but the older I get, the more I realize the key to success is taking the next step, putting myself out there for risk.

Not only did I attend Tony Robbins's seminar, but I went on to work for his company. One thing I learned from Tony is that he expects people to go home and continue to work. He expects you to listen to his CDs and take action in your life, and he wants to hear about those results. Putting in the work to further your personal development means taking on a new mindset, being open to learning, and ready for action.

Create a Plan

Once you're ready to act, it's time to set some goals. Every year since 1988, I have practiced setting annual goals. This includes determining where I want to improve in my personal development, finding two seminars I will attend, and listing the books I will read. I started with a goal of reading at least four books per year. Now it's up to 12.

Having a specific goal makes it easier to track your progress. It's important to hold yourself accountable—otherwise, you are making goals but not getting results. Find ways to integrate your new skills into everyday life. Also, remember to be adaptable. You can recalibrate your plan if certain aspects aren't working for you along the way.

Find a Mentor

Sometimes the best way to grow is to learn from others. I was able to shadow Bill and then Tony to learn from them the mindset of success. It is important that you find your own "Bill," someone whose career you admire and who can give you objective advice. If you don't know anyone, research others whose success you can replicate.

As Tony Robbins often says, "Success leaves clues." To make an effective, meaningful personal development plan, study the career path of those who have already achieved massive success and walk their talk.

How does shadowing a mentor play into your personal development plan? It's a matter of physics. Engaging a mentor creates a counterforce to balance the sometimes-hard path of personal growth. A mentor also provides a sense of stability, constructive feedback, and perspective on your goals, strengths, and challenges. Mentorship is a safe space for exploring one's weaknesses and practicing new skills without fear of reproach.

Surround Yourself with Empowering People

I learned from Bill, Tony, and others not to surround myself with negative, critical people who may try to bring me down. Negative people will make growing through personal development more challenging and success harder to come by. Instead, you want people around you who believe in you and your mission, and who make reaching your goals more feasible.

Bill told me that he had a group of businesspeople in Charlotte whom he could call on a whim for feedback. He called them his inner circle. I too have created an inner circle, a group of people outside of my mentors, people who support me, empower me, and provide advice.

I started by looking for people who had experience in five different disciplines: spiritual, physical, mental, financial, and faith. This broad yet intimate group of people has different areas of expertise and life experiences that can help me in my own personal growth.

Over the past 35 years, my inner circle has changed as people grow, move on, and pass away, but every time one member moves on, I look for another who will hold me to that standard in that discipline.

Look for Opportunities in Your Job

Sometimes, like me, you might have to reach into your own pocket to finance your personal development opportunities. Some are blessed to have great opportunities for growth through their companies. Research the options available and see if your company offers reimbursement for educational seminars or personal development training programs. Maybe you want to go through an immersive leadership training so more opportunities will be available for you in the future. The key is to look for opportunities for growth, whether it's finding ways to volunteer with your employer, taking night courses, or volunteering for a nonprofit organization, as I did with the Red Cross.

Find a Career That Fits Your Personality

If you're stuck in a dead-end job or a position you don't enjoy, you are limited in your personal development. Authentic growth comes from aligning your career with your personality, interests, skills, and goals. This starts with getting to know yourself. What is your true nature? What do you want in life, and what's preventing you from having it? Are you a natural artist, a leader, or an entrepreneur? Taking time for inner reflection allows you to leverage all your assets to make your dreams a reality.

Help Others

Have you ever heard someone say they learned more from teaching others than from going to class themselves? Helping others develop their careers is one of the most powerful strategies for developing your own career. Remember, we are all works in progress.

As you help your mentees create their personal development goals, you hone your own abilities. You also get a chance to develop interpersonal skills that are critical to success. You might even discover a career path you didn't know existed, opening new opportunities for greater fulfillment.

Personal development is crucial to achieving success and fulfillment in life, and the only way you will achieve it is to demand more of yourself than others expect from you. The steps to success start with cultivating and implementing a well-designed plan.

Personal development is not something you should do; it's something you must do. Constant and never-ending self-improvement will give you the skills and introduce you to the people who will take you to the next level.

Many people confuse personal development with inspiration. Inspiration is fine, but inspiration alone doesn't lead to action. Personal development happens when you have the discipline and motivation to learn from others and then take the action necessary to achieve the next steps.

There are always challenges along the way that life will throw at you. There are choices to make, like whether to take the new promotion even if it means moving to a new place. Those challenges aren't easy, but they help you develop and grow, and that's what determines your place, your return, your equity, and your total fulfillment and happiness.

Knowing you met the challenge is rewarding. When you face your next "personal plane crash" in life, if you have done what you need to do to prepare, you can pull yourself up and have the confidence that you can and will do it again because you have the blueprint for success.

Tom Hopkins and me at his 1992 Boot Camp

Lesson Two: Faith Moves You Forward

July 3, 1990

The day started full of great joy and hope. Terri was expecting our first child in just a few days, and both of us were so excited. We'd been getting the nursery ready and counting down the days to his due date.

We got ready for work like usual, grabbing a quick breakfast together before brushing our teeth and heading to the cars, but right before we left, Terri told me she hadn't felt our child move for a while. Being a nervous new father, I panicked, but Terri tried to put my mind at ease and said it wasn't that unusual.

She must have been more worried than she had let on, though, because at about 10:00 that morning, when I was out on appointments, I got a call from Terri. She was going to see the doctor and asked if I could meet her there. I rearranged my calendar and met her at the doctor's office.

When we got in to see the doctor, he had a concerned look on his face and recommended we go to the hospital to get checked. We went to the emergency room and checked in. After a few minutes' wait, we got in and heard the news no one wants to hear. The baby did not have a heartbeat and was dead.

It was devastating news. We thought we had done everything right. We went to classes, Terri didn't drink alcohol, she ate well, she worked out—everything the book says you are supposed to do. Why did this happen? I called my parents, Terri called her parents, and they called our siblings who rushed to Charlotte to be with us.

I didn't know what to do. There is no blueprint on what to do when you lose a child. At that time, we were visiting churches around Charlotte but hadn't found one we connected with, so, I called the office of the last one we visited and asked for the minister in charge. That church was getting a new minister; I spoke with the associate minister, and he came to our house, consoled us, and gave me guidance on what to do.

My wife and I were adamant that we wanted our child baptized before we buried him. On July 5, our son, Thomas, was delivered stillborn. He was baptized immediately upon delivery, and the next day he was buried.

I went back to work the following Monday to try to get back into my routine, but I struggled to focus. The next day, I called Bill to ask for his advice on how to handle the situation. We went out to lunch that day and I shared what happened. I told him I felt guilty. Was there something I missed or didn't do that I should have done?

To this day, I don't know what I said, but I remember the feelings I had. Bill listened intently to everything I was saying, and when I stopped speaking for a second, he offered up another of his great gems of wisdom: "Guilt serves you if you understand the purpose." I was confused, so he told me a story.

"I haven't told you this, but Bonnie and I had a son. He was drafted into the Army in 1949. We were a nation at peace, still riding high after the victory of World War II. No parent wants their child to go off to war, but it was peacetime, and like most young men at that time, he was going to do his duty. The plans after were for him to come home and learn the movie theater business.

"Then on June 25, 1950, our nation entered the Korean War. They called it a 'police action.' Bonnie was worried, but I told her there was nothing to worry about, it wasn't a war, and it was far away, way across the ocean on the Korean Peninsula. As you know from history, that police action quickly escalated into conflict, then war. Our son was dispatched to Korea. He was one of the 55,000 troops who did not return home from Korea alive."

That Bill would share his own heartbreak meant so much to me. He said, like me, he was confused and questioned if he had done everything, he could to protect his son. He felt guilty because he had the resources to possibly keep his son from having to serve in the military, but at that time, right after

World War II, so many young men felt it was their patriotic duty.

Bill said he struggled with guilt for some time, and he went to his own mentor for guidance. His mentor reminded him of his faith in God. He said the same trust in the unknown that had helped him take a risk and start a new business came from his faith in God, and that would help him in his current struggles. Faith had brought him this far and would help him and Bonnie through this. God doesn't do anything in our lives without a purpose.

Then Bill asked me if I believed in God, and I told him yes. He told me that the God who brought me into this world is the same God that Thomas was with now. I had to have faith that it happened for a reason, as God doesn't do anything without a purpose. He said this was a test of my faith, and if I could deal with this, I could deal with anything.

Later that year, Terri and I started attending the church I called the morning we found out about Thomas, and we are still there 30 years later. Our faith has been tested many times since but putting our trust in God has always helped us through. I could see that was the lesson Bill was teaching me.

We all face those defining moments in our lives, those moments when we don't know why something is happening, and we must point our trust toward the future, even when the present is such a struggle.

Fifteen months later, we had our next child, Chelsey. Maybe having a sustaining faith was the lesson I needed because God doesn't give you the lesson until you are ready.

Bill shared with me that through the years he had to call on his faith when things happened to his business and family. He had to trust that things would work out if he did everything he could, even when he could not control the circumstances—such as when he began his quest.

Bill started his business at the beginning of a nationwide depression, and no one had money to see the moving pictures he loved so much. He struggled to make payroll when his business partners let him down. Bill showed me that those challenges are all part of life. He told me to keep saying to myself, "If I can deal with this, I can deal with anything."

Like Bill, I found that my faith in God helped me in all facets of my life. Going to church with Terri was a way for our family to grow our faith and it also served me in my professional life.

At that time, I was totally committed to the goal of being the number one salesperson at my company, Automatic Data Processing. I went all in and often reminded myself that if I could deal with the setback of losing a son, I could deal with any setback. That faith served me well. For the next four years, I was a top producer in the region, and in 1994, I became one of the top five producers in the company.

When we had another child in 1993, Terri and I were doing well financially, emotionally, and spiritually, and we were enjoying raising our little family. Of course, we had setbacks at times, like everyone else, but having a strong reference for faith, we learned to survive those times and thrive.

My faith was tested in a much bigger way again a few years later. On April 13, 1997, my parents had come to Charlotte to visit their grandkids. It was a beautiful Sunday, and we had all gone to church together. After lunch, I went out to clean my gutters and my mom came out to hold the ladder for me. We hadn't talked much, so it was great to catch up and find out what was going on back home in Winchester, Virginia.

Coming out to help with chores wasn't unusual for my mom. She was one of those women who was brought up in the 1930s and 1940s when dads taught their kids how to do things for themselves. My mom was very proficient in managing a house and tools.

The next day, they left to go home to Winchester. Everything was back to normal; the kids were back at school, and I went to work. Then Tuesday night, after we'd all gone to bed, I got a phone call from my dad. My mom was watching her favorite baseball team, the Baltimore Orioles, and favorite player, Cal Ripken, Jr., when she had a stroke and was rushed to the hospital. She was lucid and awake when she got to the hospital, but the moment they put her on a table to check her out, she passed away.

My dad was devastated. He had lost the love of his life, and his life was totally turned upside down in a matter of moments.

He didn't know what he would do without my mom. He'd never had to cook, wash clothes, pay bills, or do anything around the house. After notifying my aunt, Terri's parents, and my cousins, I left for Winchester to make arrangements with my sister and brother.

After the service, Terri and the girls left for home. I hung around one more day to help my dad get some things in order, but I was in a hurry to get back home. I found myself doing the same thing I had done after Thomas was born. I went back to work, thinking that if I threw myself into my job, I would be able to ignore my emotions.

I still struggled with my concentration, so I called Bill and told him what happened. My then 90-year-old friend and mentor was still vibrant, and I knew I could count on him. We met later that week, and he reminded me that I needed to keep my faith even though I couldn't understand what happened.

"You have a family and have to be strong for them," Bill said. He helped me see that I had dealt with the death of my child seven years earlier, and I could deal with this. God doesn't do anything without a purpose. As always, I left my visit with Bill feeling stronger and able to face the challenges of life. I knew I had to work through my feelings of grief and help my family move on.

With everything going on, my wife didn't tell me she found out she was pregnant with child number three the week my mom passed away. Seven months later, our daughter Courtney was born. I started to believe that since I kept my faith after my mom passed away, maybe God gave us Courtney as a gift for believing and having faith.

As Jesus said, all it takes is faith the size of a mustard seed, and with that, you can move mountains. My faith started small, but it was that little nudge from Bill and the minister at our church after Thomas's birth that helped me begin to foster my faith in my adult life. From that point on, God continued to send challenges in my life that would test my faith, and every time I emerged stronger. I know now that those tests were preparing me for that fateful day in 2009.

The Number 15

I wasn't scheduled to be on US Airways Flight 1549. I was scheduled to be on the 5:00 p.m. flight. But when I boarded the plane earlier that day, it felt like any other flight to me. It was a typical flight, until it wasn't. I had no way of knowing how profoundly my life was about to change. I think God put me on that plane for a reason. It was my time to grow. He gave me the courage I needed to help others get off the plane and the strength to swim to the ferry. God's hand was on all of us. I believe that He was showing me that if you have faith, there is hope.

Shortly after that experience, I was interviewed on TV, and the reporter said something to me that I hadn't thought about. I was on Flight 1549, and I was in seat 15A on January 15, 2009.

She said there must be something with me and the number 15. When I got home, I looked up what the number 15 stands for in affinity numerology, and I found this: It symbolizes a concern for others, tending to nurture whenever the opportunity arises. You may become an involuntary leader, although leadership generally isn't actively sought.

I read those words and started thinking about that day in a totally different light. Maybe I was supposed to be on that plane for a reason—to nurture, grow, and learn to lead.

Where a lot of my strength came from that day, and continues to come from, is my faith. I believe that to be successful, you've got to believe in something bigger than yourself, whatever you may call it. Belief in something that will be there for you is what keeps you going when things get tough.

Challenges and setbacks will happen whether you like it or not. You don't have much control over what type of curveball you're going to get. Ultimately, what it comes down to is how you respond to each curveball, and that you have faith that it's going to work out.

Terri asked me for only two things in those early years after the Miracle on the Hudson. One was to do an interview with Rick Warren for his magazine, *Purpose Driven Connection*. One of the conditions I asked for before the interview was that the writer also interview my minister, Ken Carter, so that he could give his perspective on my faith. To this day, one of the most frequent questions I get from people is, "How has your faith changed since Flight 1549?"

I give the same answer today as I gave then: "I have always had faith and believed in a higher being, which I call God. What happened to me on January 15, 2009, was a testimonial for my faith, a strong reference, and it's imperative to have faith when things get tough."

The second thing my wife asked me to do was speak for our friend Joan at her church. Joan is a Presbyterian minister in Gastonia, North Carolina. I agreed on the condition that my wife came along to hear me speak. After the plane crash, I had been asked to speak at many churches, but Terri had never heard me speak in public.

I agreed to speak on Palm Sunday, March 28, 2010, which was our twenty-third anniversary. When I spoke at churches, which was about every other Sunday, I carried a gift that I was presented with at Oakboro Baptist Church—a matted print of the drawing of God's Hands, which had been published in the *Sacramento Bee*. It shows God's hands holding the plane up until everybody was safely off. It was an amazing way to depict that day. When I speak in the pulpit, I put it to the left of the lectern.

That Sunday was perfect—low temperatures, the sun shining brightly—and there was an overflow congregation, as it was Palm Sunday. My family was seated together. When the processional was playing, I heard the first note and started to cry. The organist played the hymn, "The Old Rugged Cross," which was my grandmother's favorite hymn. I later found out that the hymn wasn't even in the Presbyterian hymnal, and Joan had gone to a Baptist church to get the hymn!

My wife looked at me and asked, "Do you cry every time you speak?" I told her no and wiped away my tears, but I was overcome with the moment, thinking of my grandmother and how she loved the Easter season. Then it was my turn to speak. I placed the drawing of God's Hands next to the pulpit lectern and began.

When I got to the moment when I turned the drawing around for the congregation to see for the first time, it was eerily quiet. I kept speaking and then looked up and noticed a couple of young boys on my right getting up and walking down the aisle. Now, I've been a young boy in church, and I would do anything to get out of the sermon—go to the bathroom, get a drink, whatever excuse I could make—so I didn't think anything about it, but when they got to the front row, they didn't exit. They took a sharp right and stood directly in front of the drawing as I was speaking. It was even quieter than before, as the people wondered what a couple of young boys might do.

One of them interrupted me and said, "This is a miracle!" The other boy said, "He's a miracle man!"

They looked at me and turned and went back to their seats. I saw people crying in the pews and quickly looked at my wife, and she was crying too.

That was the moment she understood why I do what I do. She saw two young boys who, for at least that moment, had faith and believed in a higher being—God or Jesus. That was the moment that my faith was rewarded. You never know where destiny may take a youth, but at that moment, those two believed there is a God who does miracles.

I came away from there feeling that they now had a strong reference for faith. So, when times get tough for them, and it will, they will know that if they keep their faith, their faith will be rewarded.

Putting It into Practice

What does it mean to have faith? For me, faith is what gives me the strength to face challenges in life head-on. When I lost Thomas, my instinct was to bury my feelings in my work, but I wasn't finding success on the job and was only feeling worse emotionally. Talking with Bill helped me understand that faith in a higher power can help you work through feelings of grief, guilt, and sorrow, and through that faith, I was able to find the strength to move forward.

Figure Out What Faith Means to You

I have learned that the true meaning of faith differs from person to person. What makes life so incredible is diversity in culture, lifestyle, and faith. There are different kinds of faith, just as there are different kinds of people. Many factors go into being a person of faith and having the peace of mind that gives people of faith purpose.

Through what has happened to me in my life, I have recognized that having faith means understanding I have no control; that what will be, will be. Rather than letting that lead me to a sense of feeling out of control in my life, I have learned to put my trust in God. Faith means letting go of your worries and having a feeling of peace in knowing that your life has a purpose. Having faith means you recognize that the world does not revolve around you, that there are so many factors that come together into human life that you will never have control over and letting that be okay.

Some people find that purpose in life in Christianity, as I have. Others might practice a different religion and find that same purpose in life. If you haven't yet found a place where you feel comfortable in worship, now is the perfect time to start looking and find what faith means to you.

How You Can Implement Faith in Your Life Right Now

For Christians, baptism is an important ritual of faith, and it has been important for me on a personal level.

My parents made the decision not to baptize me in the church as a baby, which was the common practice in our denomination. Before my mom passed away, I asked her why. She told me that she wanted me to answer the vows for myself, as they would be my vows, not hers. That way, I had to live up to the vows I made. I have spoken and written about the fact that one of the best gifts my parents gave me was making me make decisions for myself and making me own them, and this was one of the biggest examples.

I was baptized as a fifth grader, and I had to answer the baptismal vows for myself. I was one of the older kids baptized that day. I took the vows of baptism and owned them for the rest of my life.

With everything going on in the world right now, the strife, anger, and uncertainty, I can't help but think of all the people who have taken the same vows. I reread the words carefully and wonder if we all lived up to just those vows we made in our lives, especially when we were baptized, would we have the challenges we see now in the world?

Getting baptized is one way to implement faith in your life, but I realize it is a very big step for some. There are other things you can do as well to help grow your faith. Something as simple as saying a prayer or an affirmation each day can help your faith grow. Ask for strength to trust in something you ardently desire that hasn't come to fruition yet, whether it be in your personal life or in your career.

I also make it a practice to never go to bed without a request from my own subconscious mind. Your subconscious mind is 30,000 times more powerful than your conscious mind. Think how powerful that is. By actively focusing on the vows you have made, both before you go to bed and when you wake up, you can manifest change in your life.

Practice Consistency in Your Faith

Depending on your circumstances, you may or may not be full of faith on any given day. Authentic faith should always be changing us in ways that only we know about. Faith isn't just a notion that you hold on to in tough times. Faith is an important element of who you are every day but holding on to that can be remarkably difficult.

Remember, faith gives us strength in times when we are weak, and it is through practicing our faith that we will grow in strength. Real faith is consistent and makes a difference when no one is watching—whether you are by yourself on a plane that is crashing in ice-cold water, or you have to make payroll and don't know how you are going to do it, or you see a loved one die and it makes no sense. God has a purpose for everything He does.

Bill showed through his example what strong faith can do in a person's life. You can put the pieces of your life back together when you start with this premise and commitment to living up to your vows, and your faith will be served. Faith is the link between you and the life of your dreams.

My baptismal class in Hillsboro, Ohio, where I was baptized at age twelve.

Lesson Three: Take Responsibility for Your Actions

September 26, 1973

I was walking down the hallway to gym class. As a new kid in school, I was still finding my way around. My family had left my childhood home in Hillsboro, Ohio, and moved to Winchester, Virginia, that August, right before school started. I was in junior high and didn't want to leave my friends and everything I knew, but I didn't have a choice.

I had managed to make friends with a boy, Captain John Smith, who had a physical and mental disability. That day, walking to gym, while trying to mind my own business and blend in, I saw a boy pushing and intimidating Captain John. Other boys were standing around watching and doing nothing.

I didn't think twice when I saw what they were doing to him. I walked up and asked the boy to stop.

"What are you planning to do about it?" he asked.

I looked around, but no one was standing up for me. Of course, they weren't I was the new kid in school, and the only people who knew me were a few others on the football team. No one else knew I was a seventh grader who had made the eighth-grade football team.

I looked at the boy and slugged him, knocking him down against the lockers. The athletic director came out and pulled us apart, sending me to the assistant principal's office. As I walked to the office, I was worried that I would get thrown off the football team, lose out on playing sports, and maybe go to detention.

"What have I done?" I thought.

When I got to the office, I waited on the hard, ladder-back chair, staring at the secretary until I was called into Assistant Principal Fisher's office. I dreaded the worst.

Mr. Fisher asked me what had happened. I told him and took responsibility for punching the boy. I also told him that I didn't like bullies, and my parents told me to stand up for those who could not stand up for themselves. I was preparing myself not only for punishment at school, but then also having to face my parents and tell them what happened. Principal Fisher thought for a second and then thanked me for sticking up for Captain John. He told me that most kids wouldn't get involved and that I did the right thing.

Mr. Fisher called my parents and let them know what happened, and that I did not get disciplined. I could go to practice and play in that Saturday's game. I was shocked and relieved. I went to practice later that afternoon, and the coach acknowledged what I did.

That was a defining moment for me. As I walked to the principal's office, I was considering whether to take responsibility for my actions or not. What would serve me better? Knowing I might get in trouble, I did what was right. I confessed, explained why I did what I did, and my behavior was positively reinforced. I learned a valuable lesson about taking personal responsibility. I started to believe that if your motives lead you to do the right thing, how can you be wrong?

That lesson usually served me well, but many years later, when I was working in Charlotte for ADP, I had my philosophy tested. On July 23, 1993, I was attending our company meeting at Callaway Gardens, celebrating the start of a new fiscal year. Our commission and bonus checks were handed out there, and we were also welcoming our new regional manager of national accounts.

I knew that I had a big year in national accounts, and I was expecting a pretty big commission and bonus check. I got $64,000, the most I'd ever received. I should have been ecstatic, but as I went up to accept my check, the new manager looked at me and said, "As long as I am here, you will never get a check this big again."

I was dumbfounded. I went through the motions, finishing the rest of the day, but as I was driving back to Charlotte, I kept thinking, "What did he mean by that?"

When I got back to Charlotte, I tried to put that suspicious feeling out of my mind. In a month we would have our

President's Club gathering, a celebration of the company's top producers. I was looking forward to enjoying another trip with my wife, as well as closing a significant sale on a new ADP product with a major new prospect in South Carolina on that trip.

Before the trip, I called Bill to check in, and I invited him to lunch. I couldn't wait to share the news about my bonus with him. When we met, he could see my excitement. I also told him what my new boss had said, and I asked him what he thought. Bill told me to watch out.

"In my experience, people like that have a personal agenda," Bill said. "You need to play everything by the book and keep your nose clean. Remember, this manager didn't hire you. He doesn't have any loyalty to you."

I took Bill's advice and went back to work, trying to dot all my i's and cross all my t's. I closed that new opportunity in South Carolina and received a lot of praise for being one of the first in the company to sell the latest technology. I felt pretty confident about what I was doing, and I quickly closed in on another substantial sale in Greenville, South Carolina.

The new technology was based in Atlanta, so I was working closely with the management group there. We finalized that agreement, and I qualified early for the next year's President's Club.

As it turns out, my regional manager was auditing everything back to 1992. That year I was with the previous management, and the new regional manager wasn't even with the company then. I was confused about why he was doing that. I called my previous manager, who was now in Los Angeles, and he was also confused.

In the audit, the regional manager found a technicality that he held me accountable for. We had signed a business deal in Charlotte, but the company's headquarters were in Washington, D.C. He claimed that I should have only received 50 percent of the commission and quota credit from that transaction, which would have knocked me out of the Board of Directors at the President's Club. That meant that I wouldn't have gotten my large bonus, and my previous manager wouldn't have received his accolades.

My new manager told me that I could resign, or he would escalate it to senior management for discipline. I contended that if the business should have been split, someone should have caught it then, and what's done is done. He said that in my employment agreement, I had agreed to take ramifications of any incorrect business. I had 24 hours to decide.

When I told Terri, she was furious. She wanted me to fight it. I also called Bill. He reminded me of what he said to me at lunch that day, that the manager had a personal agenda.

"Even if you win the fight, you will lose the war," he said.

Bill told me about a time in the 1930s when he was opening theaters so quickly and borrowing against other assets that he got overextended. Eventually, one of his loans was called.

"I didn't have the liquidity to pay off the previous loans, so the new loans were up against challenged debt," Bill said. "I was about to lose everything. I didn't know what to do, so I turned to my mentor for advice. He had never had a problem like this one, but he said, 'It's up to you to make the responsible decision. The buck stops with you.'

"My mentor said I needed to accept responsibility for my past actions, that I alone was responsible for any success I found, and not to let my history control my destiny. He said that no matter what happened, he expected me to act with integrity and within my values."

Bill reminded me of the charge from President Kennedy to the country: "Ask not what your country can do for you—ask what you can do for your country." Kennedy reminded us that it's important to take responsibility for your actions and not wait for someone else to determine your destiny. As always, I listened to Bill carefully. I had worked so hard to get where I was. Did I want to give it all up because of a new manager who had an agenda?

I couldn't sleep the entire night, tossing and turning as I contemplated my next steps. Before I went in the next morning to sit down with my boss and our personnel manager, I called the vice president, who had hired me seven years earlier, to get his thoughts. He told me that I would always have a job with him, as he knew me as a person of integrity. His advice echoed Bill's: "In the corporate world, there will be people like your regional manager with agendas, and you might win the battle, but you'll never win the war." Later that morning, I resigned.

Two weeks later, I was starting over again, this time with my former VP at another company. Letting go of the job with ADP was one of the most challenging decisions I have ever made in my life. I am a fighter, and it went against everything in me to quit, because it felt like giving up. But I learned a lot from that moment. As Bill said, "We are responsible for our past."

As the years passed, I grew to look back on that time with a new perspective. I still think I was wronged in that audit, but I'm glad I didn't fight it. If I hadn't decided to accept responsibility, even though I didn't agree, I would never have had the opportunity to grow and have the experiences I have had. Leaving ADP eventually put me on track for a job on Tony Robbins's security team, which has had a big impact on my life and, of course, the day in January on that plane, which changed the course of my destiny.

As we passed over the George Washington Bridge on January 15, 2009, heading straight for the Hudson River, I was thinking of many things including if I survived the plane crash, how was I going to get out? As you know, my game plan was to get to the aisle, go up, and get out—and then I heard my mother's voice in my head telling me, "If you do the right thing, God will take care of you." I could have chosen to put myself first and get out of the plane, but would that be right? I paused for a split second, then made my way toward the back of the plane to see if anyone needed help. I was alive, and I was going to do everything in my power to make sure others stayed alive as well.

The 36-degree water was about waist deep in the back. I got behind everyone and started to follow those in the back out of the plane. I didn't feel the water, but I could see and feel things floating in it. When I saw light at the door at seat 10F, I started to make my way out like everyone else. When I looked out, however, there was no room for me on the wing and there was no room for me in the boat. I was inside the doorway of the plane for seven-plus minutes, waist deep in water.

It wasn't my game plan to be one of the last passengers out of the sinking Airbus 320, but in life, when things start going sideways, you sometimes don't get a vote. During Covid, the entire world has been forced to adjust, be resourceful, and make life-changing decisions quickly. You don't have time to be "stuck in the doorway." You need to be able to make decisions and take responsibility for them.

Putting It into Practice

The concept of taking personal responsibility has existed since the beginning of time. At the same time, human nature has worked to try to avoid it, usually through blame shifting. Adam tried to blame Eve for his sin. Cain tried to dodge responsibility. Pilate attempted to absolve his guilt in the matter of the crucifixion of Christ. "I am innocent of this man's blood," he said. "It is your responsibility!" Ultimately, attempts to pass the buck are futile. One thing I have learned is that you may be sure that whatever you have done, you will be found out.

In 1998, I attended my first Jim Rohn seminar, and I remember him saying, "You must take personal responsibility. You cannot change the circumstances, the seasons, or the wind, but you can change yourself. That is something you have charge of." Things are coming at you, outside forces, continually challenging you, but taking responsibility starts from the inside.

Listen to Your Inner Voice

Bill and I often talked about taking responsibility. He told me that he struggled with this for many years when he was young and starting a business. He said that his mentor would never allow him to shift the blame to someone or something, that taking personal responsibility would be the cornerstone of growing his business, and people would remember that. I, too, struggled with this for a period in my life, but one day, while working as director of security for Tony Robbins in San Francisco, California, this lesson came full circle for me, and I truly understood what Bill was telling me.

We were at an "Unleash the Power Within" event. The team was performing, and things were going smoothly. We had one small incident, but it was quickly handled. As I escorted Tony to his hotel room, we discussed the incident. He reminded me that even though I wasn't directly involved with what happened, I was responsible for it, and going forward, we couldn't have anything like that happen again. I gave him my word.

Tony echoed the same lesson taught to me first by my parents, then by Bill. I'd lived it but hadn't really thought about it clearly until that moment. Going forward, I promised to take full responsibility for whatever happened in my life. Taking responsibility starts from within and will write the story of your life.

Experience, Grow, Respond

One thing I've learned from Bill, from my career, and from my other mentors is that one way to find success in life is to use personal experience for growth. Taking responsibility means taking time to assess your actions and learn from them. It also means having the knowledge and experience to help you through those times when you don't have the luxury to think before you act.

If you consider your experiences, learn from them, and incorporate that learning in your personal growth, then when you get in a situation that requires an immediate response, you'll have the ability to act quickly and do the right thing.

That moment on the plane on January 15, 2009, I had to humble myself and realize that I had to let other people use their leadership skills when theirs fit better than mine. I took a pause to grow before I responded. I became more coachable and flexible about what had to be done to survive, such as people using the seats as additional aisles to get out of the plane. In the doorway, it was a time for me to take a moment and pause so I could make life and death decisions, not only for myself, but for others. It was my liminal time, which was an uncomfortable place to be.

Make Time for Change

Right now, most of us are in liminal time. It's the time between what was and what's next. It is a place of transition, waiting, and not knowing. Liminal time is when all transformation takes place. Are you ready to humble yourself and be open so you can be transformed?

As my friend and mentor Tony Robbins says in his book *Unlimited Power*, "Change is inevitable; progress is not." Change is happening, and a strategy that I learned from my other mentor Bill, and then reinforced in 2009, serves me well today: "Attach a positive meaning to what is happening, humble yourself to be open to new possibilities and strategies, be resourceful, and take personal responsibility for your actions." When you take responsibility, and take time to learn, only then will you grow and experience success.

Joanne was our neighbor and had wisdom like Bill, and she imparted it to my daughter Courtney.

Lesson Four: No Means On

Spring 1969

It was a big time for me: the first season trying out for a competitive baseball team. In those days, there was no such thing as T-ball or coach pitch. It was just baseball. I was ready to play, but I was nervous. My mom knew it, so she spent countless hours with me in the backyard, honing my athletic abilities.

My mom was quite the athlete in her day. She was the tomboy of her family and played all sorts of sports with the boys in her hometown of Pekin, Illinois. She could pitch and catch with the best of them, and she could kick a football almost as well. In the 1940s, girls couldn't play many sports in high school, but they couldn't keep my mom off the field. She would hang around the Pekin high school baseball team and help warm up the pitchers by being their catcher in the bullpen.

Later, as an adult, she played softball and basketball on the Caterpillar industry teams in the 1950s. My mom was one athletic person. So, when it came time for me to start playing competitively, she was the one who took the time and effort to teach me the fundamentals.

That spring in our backyard, she pitched to me like she was trying to strike me out. She would hit grounders to me, hard, so I wasn't afraid of the ball. She would make me pitch until my arm was ready to drop off. She got me ready for tryouts. At tryouts, I was selected first by Hobart, the last-place team of the previous year. I was ready for a big summer, playing shortstop and pitching.

During our first practices, it was clear that I was the most skilled player on the team and could play any position. The coach, Jeff Hodson, put me behind the plate as the catcher because he didn't have anyone who could catch the pitches. I was frustrated and angry. Sure, my favorite player was catcher Johnny Bench, but I wanted to be in the field, not stuck behind home plate.

I came home ready to give it up, but my mom told me that I was not a quitter and I had to stick it out. I really pushed back on my mother. It was the first time I'd done anything like that with her, and I was letting my horrible attitude get the best of me. On the way home from practice, she and I had a heart-to-heart talk about sports and life. She told me an attitude like that was going to kill me.

"This isn't how you were raised, and you know it," she said. "I expect you to stay positive, even when you face circumstances in life that you don't like or don't agree with. Most of the time, things don't work out the way we want, but we can't let that get the better of us."

My mom gave me perspective on my negativity that set me on a path that would serve me then and for decades to come. She told me to look at it as "No means on." Anytime I started to get negative, she told me to repeat in my head, "No means on," and turn negativity into a positive. That one little lesson turned the season around for me.

It was one that propelled me in my athletic career. Not only did I have a great baseball season, but later that fall, I won the local Punt, Pass, and Kick competition and was runner-up in the district Punt, Pass, and Kick competition. It was the first of many athletic successes. My mother taught me that my attitude and being positive would take me as far as I wanted to go, and she was right.

My mother's lessons came to serve me well later, when I hit an unexpected challenge during my freshman year of college. I thought things were going well. Moving away to James Madison University (JMU) in the fall was a life-changing experience. I may have gained the freshman 15, but overall, I thought I acclimated to college pretty well. Then I went home for Christmas, and my father thought differently.

Things were different in 1979 than they are now. Grades went home to your parents instead of straight to you. When I got home, happy to be celebrating the holidays with my family, my parents had just received my grades. I knew they weren't the best, but I had passed, and I planned on doing better the second semester. My father had a different opinion. It wasn't more than an hour after I got home when my father had a come-to-Jesus talk with me. He told me that my grades were unacceptable, and if I wanted to go back to JMU in the second semester, I had to pay for it.

If there was one thing I could count on with my father, it was that he was a man of his word. I didn't know how I was going to pay for college. I had saved up money from working two jobs the previous summer, but I had spent a lot of that on having a very good time during my first semester. This wasn't how I planned on spending my winter break, but I dug down to my mom's lesson and remembered that my attitude was going to kill me unless I turned it around to the positive.

My mom and I had several talks over the holiday about my mindset and becoming optimistic and resourceful. I needed to quickly come up with $2,600 to pay tuition, room, and board by the first week of January, or I would be back in Winchester working. After working the third shift in the factory all summer while umpiring baseball in the evenings, the last thing I wanted to do was work.

My mom always told me, "Optimism is a mental habit." So, I changed my mindset. I got resourceful, called my grandmother to help me, got a loan that she co-signed, cashed out my savings, and got a job on the security team at JMU. I had to make payments back to my grandmother, but I was able to cover the costs to attend school.

For my remaining three years at JMU, I was responsible for paying my tuition, room, and board. I graduated on time through loans, working two jobs in the summers, and working at school. Without my mom's positive mindset, I might never have graduated from college, which set me up for later success.

Having a positive mindset helps you find success in sports, school, and career. I found that to be true when I was working for Business Management Services (BMS). That was the job I took after leaving ADP. I enjoyed working with Gordon, whom I'd also had the opportunity to work with at ADP. I truly enjoyed helping BMS expand and grow into new markets. I put my head and heart into my job, and it helped that the owners, Mike and Dan, treated people with respect.

They set up a compensation plan for the sales team such that if you built and serviced a business, they would pay you residuals every year that your clients stayed with BMS. I was in my second year with the company, developing the South Carolina market, when Mike called me and told me they were considering selling the company to a large firm out of Cleveland.

At first, I was excited for them, the company, and my prospects, but then Mike told me that all the sales team's agreements would be reviewed and potentially changed. When I spoke to Gordon, he told me that meant the residuals would probably go away, and the potential new company would go to a commission plan like ADP had. At first, I didn't think that would be a bad thing. Then I realized that I had built up an annual residual of $81,000 a year.

While the negotiations were going on between the owners and the Cleveland company, I was approached by PeopleSoft. In the mid-1990s, PeopleSoft was the hottest human resources, payroll, and financial system in the country. They were expanding their healthcare team and approached me about an opportunity to be a sales manager in the mid-Atlantic area. I spoke with Mike and Gordon about the opportunity, and both of them told me it sounded like a great idea.

I talked to Terri about the move, and she thought it would also be good, as it was a bigger company with lots of potential and more benefits. The next week, I accepted the position with PeopleSoft. Mike and Gordon understood, even though it was difficult telling them. They were upstanding people with a great company. A couple of months later, Mike and Dan sold BMS to the company in Cleveland, and I believed that I made the right call to move to PeopleSoft.

PeopleSoft was a new type of technology company with a more relaxed approach to business. It was people friendly and interested in developing its team on the day's new technology, which was a client server. I went from selling a service to selling software, and I had a learning curve. My typical approach to starting fast was slowed, as I needed to learn this new technology, a new set of competitors, and a new way to work with teams within an organization.

Once I learned the ropes, I started calling the hospitals in my territory. I made significant progress in getting conversations started and was traveling about four days a week. As I began developing these opportunities, I found an organization that was looking at an entire enterprise solution. West Virginia University Medical Center had older technology and wanted to surpass the other large healthcare organizations in the region. It was a great opportunity.

I knew that I had to go wide throughout the university, and I remembered what I had learned in my sales training with Tom Hopkins: "Sales is a belly-to-belly business." I went all in at a breakneck pace and was traveling to Morgantown, West Virginia, every week to make sure I could cover everything they needed.

A few months later, while in the process's final throes, I made a call to sit down with the chief financial officer and chief information officer at the university. We had a great meeting, and I felt that I did everything I could to put PeopleSoft's compelling case in front of them. Later that week, I received a phone call from the chief information officer, who said that we were selected. I was ecstatic. I called Terri and my manager, Chris. Not only was this a brand-new relationship for PeopleSoft, but it was also an enterprise solution with a substantial commission. Unfortunately, that excitement soon soured.

When we started the negotiations with the university, all was going well. We went back and forth on the points of the agreement, which is a standard procedure. We were down to a couple of final points, and when I got them, I sent them to my manager and the legal team at PeopleSoft. They both told me we would not negotiate on these points and had me go back to the university to let them know.

I did that, and I could see the goodwill that I had worked to build over the previous months was quickly dissolving. I told my manager and asked him to call the university management. He did and told them the same thing: on those two points, PeopleSoft was not willing to budge.

The chief information officer called me and thanked me for my efforts and told me they would start negotiations with the second-place company. I believe he was as sorry as I was, as we had spent a lot of time together and built a relationship, but he told me if PeopleSoft begins a new corporate relationship this way, how would they treat them once they paid for the software? I didn't have a response to that. I had to tell my manager that we were not going to get the business.

My manger was upset but told me that there were other opportunities out there and to go after them. I called Terri and was very disturbed and depressed, not only for losing an opportunity and a large commission check, but also for all the effort I put in, and that my company didn't want to go the extra mile.

I was questioning my move to PeopleSoft and wondering if I should look at changing companies. I really liked PeopleSoft and how they treated me, but these negotiations showed a new side to the company. I was getting very pessimistic in my work and started to slow my calling and prospecting. I knew it was time for a visit with Bill. He said that negotiations get messy, especially when you are looking at millions of dollars. He then shared something that happened to him when he was opening his theaters.

"Back in the '30s, the business world felt like the Wild West," Bill said. "So many people were out of work and trying to survive. I had opened up my first theater in Charlotte but was ready to expand out around Charlotte and the surrounding area."

Bill said he didn't know what to do. He thought the worst was about to happen, and he was going to lose everything. He went home to think and turned on his radio. President Franklin Roosevelt was giving one of his fireside chats. Even in the middle of the Great Depression, Roosevelt always portrayed an optimistic perspective every time he spoke to the public, including on December 7, 1941, after Pearl Harbor was bombed.

Listening to Roosevelt, Bill realized that successful people had problems like he did, but they usually succeeded if they maintained a positive and optimistic perspective. Bill got creative and found a way to repay the investor, keep his theaters, and still grow.

"It all starts with a positive attitude," Bill told me. "You can learn to practice optimism and give yourself a higher chance to achieve success, or you can stay negative and wallow in your self-pity. Optimism is an essential trait of success."

The next day, I spoke to my manager and told him that I understood the company's position. I also let him know how I felt: that we had lost a potentially important client over something that could have been negotiated.

My management was not moved by my feedback. They felt strongly that PeopleSoft had the premier software on the market and did not negotiate on key items. But one thing I learned from my personal sales training with Tom Hopkins is that people buy from people, not companies. Even though I did not finalize the sale, I kept my integrity and friendship with my client.

After that, I changed my approach with PeopleSoft. I started to refocus and called on some new hospitals in my territory, building new relationships. I also changed how I worked with the company internally, building positive relationships with our company's legal teams as I worked on potential opportunities. That way, when we got to negotiations with the new clients, the PeopleSoft legal teams were already involved and had met the new client's legal team to address these sticky issues early in the process, not at the end. I quickly closed on a new opportunity in South Carolina, and my change in attitude and approach served me well.

People often ask me how I kept so positive and rational during the events on January 15, 2009. The experiences I had in my life that led up to that moment helped me tremendously that day. As the plane headed straight for the Hudson River, there were many chances to be negative and ask, "Why me?" Throughout my life, I have learned that if I maintain an optimistic perspective, I give myself a much better chance for success.

Pessimistic people are usually right, but optimistic people are more successful. That day, success meant surviving a plane crash. To do that, everyone involved had to maintain their mindset and focus. If anyone had given up or been negative, the focus would have gone to them, not to the mission.

The reason the Miracle on the Hudson is and will be spoken about for years to come is that it showed how to bring together 155 disparate people who didn't know or care about each other and have them stay positive and optimistic. The result was a miracle. People want to believe in miracles. I believe miracles do happen, and they start by staying optimistic. The Merriam-Webster Dictionary says, "Optimism is hopefulness and confidence about the future or the successful outcome of something."

Confidence can give us an optimistic outlook, even in the most challenging circumstances. As my mother and Bill taught me, optimism is a choice. If you choose to trust God, you can rest in His promise, and He will take care of you.

Putting It into Practice

Throughout life, we all struggle when things don't go our way. Sometimes we react emotionally; I know I used to. There were times when I would snap at a referee when I believed they missed a call, or I'd get upset at a teacher when I thought I deserved a better grade than I received. When I got to high school, the varsity basketball coach, Donnie Hambleton, gave me a book, *Clyde: The Walt Frazier Story*, by Walt Frazier. I learned from the book that there are many times in life when you are not going to get the call. Still, those who face challenges and adversity rationally with optimism will have a better opportunity to succeed.

That attitude served me well many times in my life. You have to be cool in crisis times and base your actions on reason, using the best information you have at the moment. That day on the Hudson River, I felt I could keep my head and make rational decisions. Recently, we, as a world, have experienced the COVID-19 pandemic together. Throughout this worldwide pandemic, many people saw that those who maintained an optimistic perspective grew and succeeded.

Unfortunately, there were some areas in the world where even when one maintained an optimistic view, situations beyond their control prohibited them from getting the outcomes they desired. I have had that experience in my life likewise. There were times when I was optimistic and saw a vision for a positive outcome, and circumstances didn't allow me to triumph.

In those circumstances, one thing I learned that helped me was this: it's easy to blame events, but if you keep blaming events, you never give yourself the opportunity to grow!

Start Each Day with a Positive Mindset

You can learn to practice the habit of optimism, thereby greatly enhancing your chances of success, or you can choose the opposite, being pessimistic, and you can be right and be a failure.

As Bill taught me, optimism is one of the essential traits of a successful and fulfilling life. It starts with having a sense of humor, being able to laugh at yourself, being hopeful, being resilient, having a positive mental attitude, and having faith.

In his course, *The Original Science of Success*, Napoleon Hill wrote:

"You can fight pessimism through complete belief in two of the most fundamental truths of the Science of Success:

1. Whatever the mind of man can conceive and believe, the mind can achieve.
2. Every adversity and defeat carry the seed of an equivalent benefit if we are ingenious enough to find it."

Set Goals to Give Yourself Something to Look Forward To

I learned from Tony Robbins that instead of worrying about the bad things that might befall you, spend a few minutes every day focusing on the positive events that will happen tomorrow, next week, next month, and even next year. By thinking optimistically, you will find yourself laying plans to make them happen. Then, you are practicing the habit of optimism.

Find People Who Model Optimistic Behavior

Remember that no great leader or successful person was ever a pessimist. What could a pessimist promise but defeat? In addition to building an inner circle of advisors or mentors, Bill encouraged me to find leaders in every area of my life who practiced and wrote about having an optimistic mindset. It was a virtual roundtable of sorts. Mine included Abraham Lincoln, who believed that better days were to come; Franklin Roosevelt, whose optimism breathed hope into a nation in despair throughout the Depression and a world war; and Ronald Reagan, who said during the 1988 State of the Union Address, "America is, and always will be, a shining city on a hill." All world leaders who stayed positive with an optimistic perspective made a tremendous impact in the world and will be forever remembered.

Ask yourself: can you—living in the best social, economic, and political system in human history—afford not to have optimism?

Optimism attracts optimistic people. Being optimistic, in itself, is success.

Optimism is a firm belief that you can make things come out right by thinking ahead and deciding on a course of action based on sound judgment. I used references from my past to give me the certainty that I could pull off critical actions in critical moments. I had the spiritual strength to see that I could be victorious when I had no control over the events on January 15, 2009.

Learn to stay optimistic even when things don't look favorable. Weigh all factors with clear judgment. Then you can decide upon your course of action to make things turn out the way you want them.

Me proudly holding the trophy from the Punt, Pass and Kick competition when I was eight years old. It was the first time I won the PP&K competition. I went on to win it two more times.

Lesson Five:
Let Humility Guide You

April 30, 1969

My dad took me out of school early to go to the Reds game. Of course, I'd been to some games with my dad, but this one was special. I was just beginning my competitive baseball career, so I felt a real connection with the players. It was also bittersweet, because my own season started in May, and we probably were not going to be able to go to many games in the summer.

Jim Maloney was the starting pitcher for the Reds, and he was on his game. Sitting behind home plate, I could see how the pitches came in. I started learning the difference between a fastball, a curveball, and a changeup. The Reds blew the game open in a wild fourth inning, scoring seven times on the Houston Astros, so it wasn't much of a competitive game.

In the seventh inning, my dad asked if I wanted to leave.

"We could stop at Frisch's Big Boy to grab a bite to eat and get home early," he said.

"Not yet. Let's watch the Reds bat one more time."

At the end of the seventh inning, he asked again, but when we both looked up at the scoreboard, we noticed that Maloney was pitching a no-hitter. I had never seen a no-hitter.

We both agreed we should stay. "We'll go if he gives up a hit," I said.

We stayed through the eighth inning, and the no-hitter was still intact. When the Reds came out for the top of the ninth inning, there was a murmur throughout the small crowd at Crosley Field. Every pitch carried a little more anticipation. With two outs, Jimmy Wynn got a walk, and Doug Rader came up to the plate.

The more baseball you watch, the more you understand that you cannot give free passes. At this point in the game, it was no longer about which team won or lost but about making a historic no-hitter. The crowd held its breath on each pitch. Maloney had Rader at two balls and two strikes. On the next pitch, Rader struck out. The no-hitter was complete. The players flooded the field. My dad and I had a great view of it all, right there behind home plate.

During all that celebrating, I noticed something. Even with all that was going on, Johnny Bench went up and shook Maloney's hand with little fanfare. He showed grace and humility, which was a trait of Johnny Bench and was why I always gravitated to players like him.

My mother always told me that in victory, people will notice how you act, which is why it's important to always show humility. You never achieve success alone. It's always a team effort, whether it's your ball team or your family or your group of friends. If you look at the players whom I have followed intently throughout my life, they all have that trait.

It's too bad my dad and I didn't get to go back the next day. After Maloney fired the last Reds' no-hitter in Crosley Field, the Astros' Don Wilson pitched a no-hitter against the Reds. Wilson's second career no-hitter marked the last one thrown at Crosley Field and the second time in big-league history that two teams no-hit each other in successive games.

This lesson on teamwork that I learned from Johnny Bench was only the first of many I would experience from different coaches and mentors over the years. The next time came at the Jerry West Basketball Camp at the Virginia Military Institute. When I attended that camp, I was fortunate to be picked to have a special small group shooting lesson with Jerry West.

I idolized Jerry West, not only for his talent, but for his attitude and character. He came from a small town in West Virginia and was always all about the team. A group of us sat on the floor on the main court at VMI watching Jerry. While he was shooting (and not missing much), he was talking about playing at the pro level and having the mindset of a pro.

He was more focused during that session about the mentality of a champion rather than on the skill set of shooting. As I listened, I learned that I needed to focus more on getting my team involved and getting my mind right before I practiced and played. When I shook his hand at the end, he looked me in the eye and said, "Thank you for coming." He was genuinely gracious and thankful for the opportunity to impact youth, and that really made an impression on me.

The next year, I was invited to attend the Gale Catlett basketball camp at the University of Cincinnati. It was a dream come true for me, as I grew up right outside of Cincinnati and it was like going home. When the coaches picked the teams, I was selected to be on one of the better teams. The day before the end of camp and the final games, we had a surprise. Oscar Robertson showed up at the camp to give a clinic.

When I was growing up in Cincinnati, Ohio, Robertson was the man. Getting to the NCAA final four twice, winning an Olympic gold medal, and being first selected in the NBA draft, Robertson changed the game of basketball. He was the first big point guard who could score from anywhere, pass, rebound, and play tenacious defense.

As Robertson took the court to speak to the campers, he asked for a volunteer to play one-on-one with him. I quickly raised my hand and was selected. I jumped up and ran to the court. As Robertson dribbled and started talking, my job was to guard him. He had a signature move where he would put his backside into you to move you back, then step back and shoot.

The first time he did it on me, he got around me and swish. The next time, I knew what he was going to do, and I pushed back on him. He got a little more forceful, and swish again. The final time I was determined not to let him score, so when he pushed back toward me, I stood firm. He wrapped his arm around me and scored. Then he looked at me and smiled.

"Kid," he said, "you did great. Focus on your defense as much as you do your offense, and you'll really stand out as a player." He shook my hand and finished up.

When my dad picked me up from camp the next day, I told him about that experience. Robertson had reinforced in me that great players work on all aspects of their game with humility.

Years later, while traveling to Pittsburgh, Pennsylvania, for a business meeting in 2011, I looked up and saw Robertson walking through the airport. I went up to him and reminded him of the camp in 1974 and thanked him for what he said to me. He looked at me and thanked me for remembering.

"What do you do for a living now?" he asked.

"I work for Oracle, and I also do motivational speaking. I was one of the 155 people who survived the Miracle on the Hudson. That really changed my life."

Robertson was amazed. "What do you think was the factor that led to your survival that day?" he asked.

Without a second thought, I knew the answer to that. It came down to teamwork and people checking their egos at the door. Robertson smiled, and we shook hands and went our separate ways. Who would have known that an encounter in 1974 would come full circle 37 years later, when I could share that a lesson, I had learned from an all-time player about humbling myself paid off in such a big way?

Teamwork isn't only important in sports. It's a factor of success in your career as well. I learned that for myself when I went to work for Modern Office Machines. I had just gotten married and had quit what seemed to be a sure thing in the restaurant business to take a job selling copiers door-to-door in west Charlotte. It was a scary time, but I knew I needed to take the chance.

I knew nothing about sales, but I thought that if I was going to learn, the best way was to start with the most basic of sales: door-to-door. Modern Office Machines took a chance on me and told me that if I put in the time and effort and did not quit, they would train me, and I could succeed.

That first sales job was on straight commission with a draw. At first, I didn't understand what a draw against commissions was, but at least I had income coming in. The company gave me a great trainer who traveled up from Greenville, South Carolina, each week to spend time in the field with me.

It turns out that I had to get a copier to carry with me so I could demonstrate it for customers. If I didn't sell it, I had to bring it back and check it out again the next day. Immediately, first day on the job, I was already in debt from buying a van. Then, on top of that, I faced a lot of rejection in my first days in sales. They said you shouldn't take rejection personally, but I was.

I was a pretty good hotel/restaurant manager, but the rejection in that business was nothing compared to being thrown out of offices. One day, after being told no yet again, I was extremely dejected and didn't know what to do. Did I make a huge mistake? Should I go back to hotel/restaurant management? Get a job behind a desk? I called Bill, and we met at Howard Johnson's for lunch.

I detailed the rejection and the doubt I was having to Bill, and he sat and listened. Then he asked me a few questions.

"Do you really want to go back and start over in restaurants? Or do you want to have a chance to take ownership of what your true worth is?" he asked.

"Back in the '30s, I thought things were going great. I'd opened up my first theaters and was on top of the world but then we got to a point in the Depression here in Charlotte when suddenly people had to make a decision—go to the theater or eat."

Bill had thought he had everything going his way, but then circumstances out of his control began to affect his success. He turned to his mentor for help.

"We met, and he told me that he was proud of what I'd achieved, but that I needed to be careful. He said that while being a leader in your field is a positive thing, sometimes it leads to being overconfident.

You might start to believe your approach is the best or the only way to get things done. But if you do that you may miss out on new ideas, fail to anticipate the future, and narrow your thought process. The best leaders avoid falling into this trap by learning to humble themselves and committing to constant learning and growth.

Continually check your ego at the door, seek out new ideas, and revisit your assumptions about how to go about your business. Get around people who don't look and think like you. Ask your younger employees to share their thoughts and point out key insights you may be missing. Set aside time to reflect on what you've learned from them, especially those whose focus and experience are different from yours and don't let your expertise be your affliction!"

Bill told me that once he started to humble himself and ask for help from his employees and his burgeoning roundtable, he began to be more creative in his outlook.

His team came up with the idea of not charging people to attend the movie theaters but charging them a nominal fee for popcorn and soda. That way, they could eat and see a moving picture.

"If I hadn't humbled myself to go to my mentor, George, and ask for help and then bring in his team of friends and employees, I may not have made it through those tough years," Bill said.

After talking with Bill, I decided to stick with selling copiers door-to-door, but I humbled myself and asked my trainer, Matt, for help. Matt spent a lot of time with me, working with me before, during, and after hours. I started to sell copiers every week and became a salesperson of the year. If I hadn't sat down with Bill and learned to humble myself and ask for help, I may have never stuck with sales and had the success I have.

After surviving the plane crash on January 15, 2009, I was inundated with requests for interviews, even as the nurses and doctors were working on getting my vitals back in line. Late that evening, the doctors made the call to limit the number of media personnel allowed in to see me. I had not spoken with my wife, as I was still in recovery, and I had lost my phone in the Hudson River.

About 11:30 p.m., Gary Mignone, the public relations director at Palisades Medical Center, came into the ER room and asked if I wanted to take a phone call. I asked him who was calling, and he told me it was Tony Robbins. I told him I would take the call.

That week I had traveled from Sarasota, Florida, to Petersburg, Virginia, to Brooklyn, New York. We were going into walk-in freezers, and I needed a heavy coat, so I packed the jacket I'd been given when I was Tony's security director. During the rescue, when I got to the triage center in Weehawken, New Jersey, that coat was taken from me as it was soaked with ice-cold water, and I didn't know if I would ever see it again. I knew once someone saw it and saw my name on the front, they would put two and two together.

When I picked up the phone, the first thing I wanted to let Tony know was that I had had my security coat on, that it was taken from me when they took all my clothes off, and in the event someone called his office, they should know so they could handle it.

"You may start getting calls from the media, as I was on about every major channel," I said.

Tony laughed his deep laugh and told me that was how his team found out that I was on the plane, as one of his people saw my interview with Katie Couric. He said he was calling to ask how I was doing, not to follow up on his jacket. He told me not to worry, that he would be honored to handle it personally, and we spoke for another 15 minutes or so. At the end of that call, he told me to call him later, as he wanted to coach me on how my life was about to change.

Later that evening, Tony put out a YouTube video about that call, which I later saw. I got very emotional when I saw it, as Tony spoke from his heart about me and our relationship.

A couple of weeks later, I was asked to go to Los Angeles, California, to do interviews on some shows. Knowing that Tony lived in Palm Springs, I called him and told him I'd be in California. He asked me to call him when I got there. When I got to California we met up, and Tony had a lot to share. He had been doing this for over 30 years, and I wanted his knowledge and experience. One thing he told me was to stay humble.

"Don't let all this hype go to your head," he said. "Success is always a team effort, and it's important to always give credit to the team. Also, when someone gives you credit, always turn it around to thank the team. Stay humble."

Those couple of hours with Tony were indeed a gift to me. Tony Robbins, my mentor and a master at his career, reinforced what I'd learned from my parents, coaches, and Bill, which was the importance of focusing on humility. Success is never about what you have done as an individual.

Even when you don't think you have a team around you, someone is always there to be your wingman. What I learned from the hall of fame athletes and leaders starting in 1969 from Johnny Bench, in 1973 from Jerry West, in 1974 from Oscar Robertson, in 1986 from Bill, and in 2009 from Tony was consistent and accurate.

Don't let your expertise be your affliction. Always be humble but not timid. The challenge of personal leadership is how to maintain the high standards you set for yourself, regardless of what others may do or say. Success without humility will be temporary and unfulfilling.

Putting It into Practice

Have the Humility to Prepare, So You Have the Confidence to Execute

I have always believed in preparation. Being a student athlete helped reinforce that characteristic.

When my family moved to a new state the year, I started junior high, I gravitated toward the athletic department to try to fit in. I was chosen for the eighth-grade team as a seventh grader. Taking a position on the team away from boys who'd grown up in that town made things a little difficult, to say the least.

Luckily, my basketball coach was also the guidance counselor. He took me under his wing. As he and I spoke, he started telling me about how he followed John Wooden and his Pyramid of Success. I started studying it and began following Wooden's teachings as well. It taught me many lessons, but one that has served me over and over is that those who succeed have the humility to continuously prepare.

Practice, Practice, Practice

Sometimes people think preparation is something you can do quickly, like reading over notes before a talk or doing some quick research on Google before a big presentation. I have learned that shortcuts don't lead to success. Preparation is about more than doing the research. It's about doing the work to improve.

When I was asked to speak at the Secret Service Summit in Cleveland, Ohio, I was worried I didn't have what it takes to be part of that panel of experts. The Secret Service Summit is the premier conference in the country to help companies make massive improvements in their customer service skills. I was honored to be asked to speak alongside an all-star cast of speakers, each with actionable messages about customer service.

I used a quote from my earlier days in sales to motivate me:

Don't prepare until you get it right—prepare until you can't get it WRONG!

Kenneth Van Barthold

Devote the Necessary Time to Prepare

One of my goals as a speaker was to be selected to present a TED Talk. When I was chosen to do my first TEDx Talk at Queen's University in Kingston, Ontario, I was not only honored but also a little nervous. I had watched a TEDx Talk online and marveled at the succinct way the presenter was able to articulate their message. Speakers only have 18 minutes to present their big idea. For someone who delivers keynotes that average 50 minutes, figuring out how to get my message out in 18 minutes was a daunting task.

I reached out to people in my inner circle who'd done a TED Talk. Most of them told me to plan on spending about five hours in preparation per section of the talk to get it squared away and down to the 18 minutes. Tony Robbins had taught me to "know your content so well you speak from the heart," which made preparing that much a challenging thought. I wanted to be congruent with the message I wanted to share, which was "model yourself on those who have the result you want, and if you do exactly what they do, you too will obtain that outcome."

I went back to what I learned in seventh grade from John Wooden and humbled myself and invested the time to prepare. When I went to rehearsal before I presented and I saw the other TEDx speakers, I did not want to be the one who stood out for not being prepared. The rehearsal didn't go as smoothly as I wanted, so I stayed up all night, making sure I couldn't get it wrong. I presented my TEDx Talk, "Bouncing Back: An Experience with Post-Traumatic Growth Syndrome," and the preparation I invested in it paid off. It went flawlessly.

The lessons I learned as a young student athlete have served me to this day. When it is essential to you, you must have the humility to prepare; then you will have the confidence to execute in the moment.

This was at Tony's last one-day Competitive Edge event held in Tampa, Florida. I was his assistant head of security at this time.

Lesson Six:
A Vision of an Alternative Future

January 23, 1972

For my eleventh birthday, my mom purchased my first Boy Scout uniform. This was a big moment in my life because it marked going to Scouts with the big guys. I had been in Webelos and was excited to graduate to the Boy Scouts.

Later that week, I went to my first Boy Scout meeting and met the scoutmaster, Lawson Walker. Mr. Walker was very passionate about Scouting. He made it sound like the adventure of a lifetime. He shared information about the camping trips, Jamborees, and service opportunities that Scouting had to offer.

Mr. Walker also shared that he was one of the first Scouts in Highland County, Ohio, to earn the distinguished Eagle Scout Award. I couldn't wait to get started. I signed up that evening.

When I got home, I ran in and told my mom I was going to be an Eagle Scout. My mom was very excited for me and glad to see me take an interest in Scouting, but she also talked with me about how Scouting was a commitment and she expected me to take it seriously. She told me to write down that I wanted to be an Eagle Scout. I believe that was the first goal I ever made.

Troop 171 met at a fort in the woods behind our house, so I could walk to the meetings. I was very excited and curious and asked Scoutmaster Walker a lot of questions. He picked up on my interest rather quickly and began to pay a lot of attention to me. He helped me put together a plan to get my Eagle Badge and told me I would need 21 merit badges to earn Eagle.

I got to work right away, working on merit badges on topics I already had some knowledge of, such as swimming and family life. Each week I spent time at the meetings reviewing with the scoutmaster what I had to do and quickly ranked up, earning my Tenderfoot, then Second Class, then First Class ranks. I attended my first summer camp and earned additional merit badges. I wanted to be the youngest ever in Highland County to earn my Eagle Scout Award.

Once I earned my First-Class rank, I moved to the second phase, which focused more on personal growth and team leadership. I also focused on the merit badges required to earn Eagle. Every week I would go by Scoutmaster Walker's house, we would discuss how I would earn these badges, and he found additional opportunities to help me develop my leadership skills.

I was learning a lot at this age, not only from Scouting but also from participating in athletics and school activities. Time management became my best friend. As I started to get deeper into the required merit badges, Scoutmaster Walker would mentor me and introduce me to local dignitaries to help me with badges for local and community citizenship.

I met the mayor of Hillsboro, Ohio, civic leaders in Kiwanis and Lions Clubs, and council members. My mom kept tabs on my work, making sure I honored my commitments and showed up for each of these introductions. When we got to the Citizenship in the Nation merit badge, which is one of the required and core badges to the Eagle Scout, my mom got more involved. She grew up in Pekin, Illinois, and had a friend, Joy Dirksen, who lived on her block. Joy was the daughter of Senator Everett Dirksen and the wife of Senator Howard Baker from Tennessee.

My mom made the call to her lifelong friend and introduced me to Joy and her husband. That was the first time I had the opportunity to meet a national political leader. Senator Baker was gracious, taking time to answer some questions and help me with my requirements for the Citizenship in the Nation merit badge. I was on the fast track to Eagle.

As I progressed to Eagle, I was also going for other leadership distinctions—the God and Country and Order of the Arrow designations. I was all in for Scouts, and it looked like I was on track to becoming the youngest Eagle Scout in Highland County history. Then, my father came home and told us he had accepted a promotion at work. We were going to move to Virginia.

I was so upset. I was getting ready to go to Scout camp to earn more merit badges, and I was finishing up my God and Country award. This news could not have come at a worse time. I had just become a Star Scout and was making tremendous progress to my Life badge. Eagle was within sight. My dad told me that we wouldn't move until after the end of the summer so I could complete my baseball and Scouting commitments.

I know that was tough on my dad. He spent the summer commuting from Ohio to Virginia. He understood how big this move was for our family and knew I had many activities that needed to be completed in about six months. I earned my God and Country award and later that spring my Order of the Arrow, but there was no way I would get my Eagle in that time frame.

I went to Scoutmaster Walker's house to talk with him. He was also disappointed, but he told me that he would make a call to a troop in Winchester, Virginia, and make it easier for me to get involved and get my Eagle.

Before I left for Virginia, I met with Mr. Walker again. Before we said goodbye, he pulled out a medal and gave it to me.

"Son, this is the medal my father got when he returned home in 1918 from serving in World War I," Mr. Walker said. "He was honored for his service and for keeping his faith in battle. I want you to have this, to remember me and the troop." I was overcome with emotions. I started to cry, even though Boy Scouts don't cry! I still have that medal, and one day I will pass it on as he passed it on to me.

Things changed when I moved to Virginia. Scoutmaster Walker had followed up on his promise and sent me with an introduction to Ben Cain, the troop master in my new town, but I just never found the same enthusiasm for Scouts after the move.

I was further along on my path to Eagle than other Scouts my age in the troop, so Mr. Cain looked to me more as a mentor and a leader, while he focused on bringing the other boys along on their rank. I went to camporee, summer camp, and even a Jamboree, but without a Scouting mentor like Mr. Walker, my energy was waning.

In addition, I was becoming more active in sports. I played a sport each season and was working hard to acclimate to a new school and new friends. My mom reminded me of the goal I'd set when I was 11, but it wasn't her job to get to Eagle—it was mine.

In the spring of 1976, I told my mom and dad that I was going to give up Scouting to focus on high school sports. My mom was devastated. She said that this decision would stay with me the rest of my life. I only lacked four merit badges and a service project to get my Eagle. She knew how close I was and that it was a life-altering decision, but I didn't believe her at the time.

I had lost my passion, ambition, and drive to get my Eagle rank. To this day, that decision to give up on that goal is the worst and most devastating decision I have ever made. I vowed that I would never again stop on the five-yard line when I was so close to scoring and achieving my goals.

In 1989, I started a tradition for Bill and KL. Between Thanksgiving and Christmas, I invited him to lunch. It was a way for me to thank him for being there for me, and it provided time to connect and catch up.

I had a pretty good year in 1989. Terri and I were in our first house, both employed, doing pretty well financially, and expecting our first child. As we were having lunch, we talked about the new president, George Bush, and how he would be able to carry on what President Reagan started.

At lunch, Bill gave me a history lesson. I knew that President Franklin Roosevelt inspired Bill because of the things he told me about the fireside chats he listened to in the 1930s and 1940s. What I didn't know was that he met President Roosevelt in person in 1938!

Bill told me that President Roosevelt was just like he was on the radio, approachable and amiable. He was focused and optimistic. He told me that he could feel the passion President Roosevelt had for being president and helping people.

"I was only around him for a couple of minutes, but I left inspired," Bill said. "Just hearing the passion behind Roosevelt gave me passion for my own business. I felt like if I could keep my love for what I was doing, I would be successful."

Roosevelt wasn't the only president Bill met. He got the opportunity to meet President Reagan in 1980.

"Reagan was gracious but serious," Bill said. "He was focused but adaptable. I also could tell he was amiable and wanted to get to know you as a person. He wanted to understand how he could help people. They were both different in their own ways, but I saw some similarities between the two men."

"What did you see that made you think that?" I asked.

"Both of the men were able to find a way to turn their weaknesses into strengths," Bill replied.

Bill went on to explain some of the other similarities he saw between the two men. Both presidents valued loyalty and competence; both were able to distinguish between foreign policy, domestic policy, and energy policy; and both could focus and make decisions based on their one-world view, which encompassed all policies from a holistic perspective.

When they made decisions, they leaned into their faith. Because of that, they never wavered. They knew their decisions were based on a higher calling. Bill also said that he learned that both President Roosevelt and President Reagan relied on an inner circle of people who gave them guidance in tough times.

We finished up our lunch together, and as always, I felt like I'd learned so much. Then Bill added to it with this last bit of knowledge that he had learned from his own mentor, and he felt was reinforced in his interactions with the presidents: "Always have work worth doing and do it extremely well, with passion."

Roosevelt faced Nazi dictatorship versus freedom. Reagan faced communism versus freedom. Both were faced with good versus evil, which is a primary tenet of believing in something bigger than yourself. Both were passionate about their worldviews. Both had a vision for an alternative future, and both will be remembered as great presidents.

That day, I received a first-hand history lesson of two great presidents. That conversation is embedded in my head and heart. I learned a great deal about personal leadership and how passion can not only drive you, but also set you on your pathway to your destiny. That is why both President Roosevelt and President Reagan are in my personal virtual roundtable.

I had passion for Scouts, and at just 11 years old, I had set a goal for myself, but when I lost my trusted leader, I lost some of that passion. I failed to meet my goal, but I wonder sometimes, what would have happened if I'd had the opportunity to stay where I was inspired by a great leader?

Bill found inspiration in Roosevelt and Reagan, as did many other Americans. Those lessons imparted to me by Bill came back to me 20 years later, when I was faced with my own challenge in becoming a leader to others.

It was January 18, 2009, three days after the Miracle on the Hudson. I had survived 36°F (2°C) water on an 11°F (–11°C) day. My story was one that inspired a lot of people, and I was being followed by the media everywhere I went. The day I got home from Palisades Medical Center, reporters from CBS followed me to my daughter's varsity basketball game. I spoke with the principal at Myers Park, and he told me that as long as they paid for their tickets, he would allow them in, but he would keep them at a distance so as not to disrupt the game.

That was just one example. Every time I left the house, I knew I was being followed. On Sunday, I was asked to go to a 7:00 a.m. service at a Baptist church in Weddington, North Carolina, to say a few words. As I expected, a local TV station showed up.

When I left Weddington to go to my church, I requested that if they were going to follow me, to please stay outside in the parking lot, as I didn't want to disrupt the services.

They agreed. When I got to my church, I was being stopped every few feet by fellow congregants. When I got to my seat with my family, the parishioners around us were talking. Right before the processional, a gentleman came up and asked me if I would speak at a men's breakfast the next Sunday. I felt boxed in. I felt as if I couldn't say no to someone at my church, so I told him I would do it.

That following week was hectic, as I went back to work, which was a decision I wish I had the opportunity to make over again. I was being interviewed three or four times a day by media from all over the world. I hardly had time to concentrate on my job responsibilities, let alone prepare for the men's breakfast.

When Saturday arrived, I completely forgot about my commitment. The men's breakfast chairman called our house. Terri picked up the phone, as I didn't want to answer any calls, and took the message. She reminded me that I agreed to speak at church the next morning. I didn't overthink it. I hadn't prepared, but it was a men's breakfast at my church. What could happen? It's just 50 old guys eating pancakes.

The breakfast was scheduled for 9:15 a.m. I got there a few minutes early, and when I showed up, there were about

400 or 500 people already there. They had moved the breakfast to the gym to accommodate the overflow. I asked the leader what happened, and he told me they had advertised it in the paper. They didn't expect that many people and didn't have enough pancakes to serve. I started thinking, was this what it was like when Jesus fed the 5,000? Was food going to show up magically?

I was a little flustered, as I didn't prepare, and I didn't have any idea what I was going to say. I went out behind the curtain into the hallway and prayed to God: "God, please give me something to say." After they said their opening prayer and people were served, it was my time to speak. I said another prayer in my head and started talking.

I didn't know what I was saying, but I saw people crying, and they were as quiet as church mice. I spoke until about 10:30. Many people came up to me when I was done and shook my hand, hugged me, and some ladies who attended the breakfast kissed me on my cheek. I didn't know what was going on. Two men came up and wanted to speak with me. They were both members of our church. One worked at Wachovia and the other at Bank of America. Both had associates who were also on the plane, and they had questions.

As we were talking, I looked up and saw an elderly lady staring at me. I had never seen her at our church before. When she caught my eye, she started to make her way up to see me. She came up on my left, interrupted our conversation, and grabbed my left arm.

The two men went silent. I was startled and jumped back, but she held firm. Then she looked in my eye and said something that changed my destiny. She said, "I don't believe in God, and I don't believe in miracles, but you … you … you are physical evidence there is a God, and He does miracles. Thank you. Thank you!" She looked at me one more time, squeezed my left arm, and walked away.

I have never seen that lady again, but I looked at the two men, and they were crying out loud. I had never seen men cry like that in public. My minister witnessed this from afar; I looked at him and that was when I realized my mission and my passion.

That elderly lady, who would soon see her Maker, now believed that there is a God who does miracles, because I am physical evidence that there is a God. It's like the story of Thomas not believing what Jesus said until he had physical evidence. This lady needed physical evidence that miracles do happen. At that moment, I represented a miracle. We all can be a miracle to someone if we live with a passion for our mission.

Putting It into Practice

Bill had the opportunity to meet two great men, President Roosevelt and President Reagan. Their passion for helping and their ability to lead others is beyond inspiring. Not everyone will become president of the United States, but we all have the opportunity to shape our destinies by following our passions.

This is something that I learned at an early age when Scoutmaster Walker became my mentor. His passion for Scouts inspired me, and I set goals for myself that shaped the rest of my life. I might not have been able to follow through with the Eagle Scout Award, but I learned many valuable lessons on leadership and community service during my years as a Scout. That passion for Scouting helped me focus and learn from my experiences.

The same can be done in your life. Your passion will drive you and can also set you on your pathway to your destiny. You may be on a specific path in your life. You may be happy and prosperous, but if you don't have passion for that path, you will never truly be fulfilled.

Find Your Distinct Advantage

Many people ask me, "How do I know where my passion lies?" I say, look to the defining moments. There are defining moments in your life that reveal what your mission and passion are, what you are uniquely gifted for. This is what I call finding your distinct advantage, and it is what I am most passionate about.

I have spent my life training for this role without really knowing it. Through sales, management, and security jobs I learned valuable skills in working with other people, inspiring them, and getting a message across. Then January 15, 2009, happened.

That day showed me what I was uniquely gifted for and most passionate about. That was the Point In Time That Changed Everything for me. In baseball terms, it is my PITTChE! You, too, will realize your PITTChE once you find your distinct advantage.

Stay Steadfast to Your PITTChE

After the Miracle on the Hudson, I was in the green room at *Good Morning America* with other passengers after our interview. There was a passenger who approached me and was upset. He told me that he never wanted to see or be with this group again, and he stormed out.

At first, I thought, "What's wrong with this guy? We survived a plane crash, and we are on national TV. We are blessed beyond blessed." What I found out later was he had lost his job and he was getting a divorce. He blamed both on what happened to him during and after the Miracle on the Hudson. The meaning he attached to that experience was devastation.

I started thinking: How many times in my life have I judged someone so quickly before I knew their backstory that it cost me relationships, job opportunities, or advancement? If I could pause and be less judgmental in the future, how would my life change? If I changed my worldview to be less judgmental, how could that affect the course of my life?

I started to change my worldview not to judge people until I understand their entire circumstances and backstory. That one thing—adapting, implementing, and not wavering from that worldview—has changed the direction of my life and has opened up so many more opportunities and relationships.

Set Goals

Once you have pinned down your passion, as I did with my new worldview, use that to help you set goals. I knew I wanted to continue to share my experiences, because I felt that what I had learned could help others. I made a goal to present a TED Talk. I didn't know how to go about doing it, how to apply, or where to apply, but I was committed. As I started looking into it, the first one that popped up was a TEDx Talk at the University of Santa Clara. I applied and then waited.

I received an email stating that I had made it to stage two. I was excited and expectant. A couple of weeks later, I received an email saying that I did not make the final cut, and to apply again next year. I was a little down, but after being in sales for over 30 years, I wanted to find out what I could do better next time. I called the person in charge, and he took my call. We spoke for about 10 minutes, and he coached me on what I could do to improve my chances. I thanked him and took his advice.

After that, I applied to ten TEDx Talks, and within a week, four of them offered me an opportunity to present. I responded to the one at Queen's University in Kingston, Ontario. My team was based in Toronto, Ontario, and I wanted them to be involved.

In my TEDx Talk, "Bouncing Back: An Experience with Post-Traumatic Growth Syndrome," I showed how you can grow from the traumatic life experiences that you will encounter, like the one all of us are experiencing during this worldwide pandemic. Knowing, writing down, and implementing your worldview, the thing in life that you are passionate about, can give you your date with destiny and set for you a new vision for an exciting alternative future.

Receiving my God and Country Boy Scout award from Scoutmaster Walker. He was very influential in my life.

Lesson Seven: Find Your Focus

August 26, 1977

The first game of my sophomore football season was ready to kick off, and I was prepared to go. I had worked out all summer, did what the coaches asked, and was named the starting center and punter. The coaches thought I was undersized for a center, but I was quick and could get to the block.

That first game at center was a little rough, but I had a good punting game, and we won. The head coach, Jerry Kelican, asked me to come early to practice on Monday to get some additional reps in. I went but I wasn't as sharp as I should have been. That Thursday, our offensive line coach, Coach Cobb, told me he was going to start a senior for our next game, as he was bigger, and they needed someone with more "meat" in the middle.

I was disappointed, but my dad told me to get my mind right and work harder in practice. The next Monday, I went to practice with a new resolve. I didn't win the starting position back, but I was still the starting punter and was punting well. I knew if playing in college was going to be an option, my work ethic had to pick up. I had to be on the field every down.

During practice the next week, my effort and focus picked up, and I was going full out. As I was pulling down the line to my right to reach a block, someone on the first-team defense went low and hit me directly on my knee, and I went down. I had never felt anything like that, as I had never been injured.

The coaches yelled at me to get up and do it again, but I could barely stand and hobbled to the sideline. The third-team center came in, and Coach Cobb came over and asked me if everything was alright. My knee was throbbing, and it turned black and blue. He told me to put some ice on it and hang in there. At the end of practice, when we ran sprints, I tried to run but struggled.

Coach Kelican came over and asked me if I needed help. My dad always taught me to man up and not let anyone see when I was hurting, so I told Coach I'd be there tomorrow. He told me to meet the team doctor in the locker room. When I reached the locker room and the team doc, he told me to go to the emergency room and get it checked out. I drove myself to the hospital and got X-rays. I found out that I had severely strained knee ligaments, and they put a cast on my leg. Since this was my left leg, I struggled to get in the car and then drove home.

My mother was furious with the coach and with me. She couldn't believe that the coach would let me drive myself to the hospital and was mad at me for driving her car with a leg I could not bend or put pressure on. I was disappointed, as I knew my season was probably over, and now I was also in jeopardy of missing time on the varsity basketball team. I couldn't even travel with the team to the next away game at Woodbridge. I was mad and depressed.

The next five weeks went slowly as I tried to get back to the team as soon as I could. In 1977, there wasn't much in the way of rehab, and my recovery went slowly. My mother kept telling me to keep my head in the game and stay focused on getting better. She knew that basketball was my real love at that time, and I had a chance to start that season. I worked hard and got back to the football team in the ninth game, but I didn't play that game or the final game.

I was working my way back into shape to play basketball, but my leg had atrophied and was weak. It was my left leg, my push-off leg for jumping, and I was struggling to rebound and play defense, which was what I was known for. In my junior basketball season, I was the seventh man. I played just about every game but didn't log many minutes. My stats were limited, and now I knew I might not be able to play in college. My attitude was suffering.

My mom kept telling me my attitude was going to kill me. She told me I needed to get rid of my pity party and get focused. She suggested I visit my old coach, who was now the varsity coach at Martinsburg High School in West Virginia.

I went to Martinsburg to see Coach Rogers. When I moved with my family to Virginia, sports were the way I adjusted to a new life. At that time, Rogers was the head high school coach there. Though I wasn't in high school yet, he met with me during my first week of school in Virginia and was my biggest cheerleader. He coordinated the camps I went to at the University of Cincinnati.

When I was in tenth grade, he took a head coaching position at Martinsburg High School in West Virginia. I was devastated. I had been looking forward to playing for him in my high school career. He told me to stay in touch and call on him if I ever needed anything. Now I was taking him up on that.

When I met with Coach Rogers, he gave me great insights on what I needed to do. First, he said, I needed to get my head on right and focus on what I wanted, not what the circumstances were. There it was again—the advice to get focused. I went home energized and put a game plan together to have an outstanding senior year in sports.

That summer, I worked harder than I had ever worked. I got focused. I got my first job, umpiring baseball, and worked out every day. Don Shirley was the principal at James Wood High School, and he and I were friends; he would open the weight room for me every day so I could lift. I joined the summer track league and ran the distance runs as well as competed in long jump and triple jump, so I had endurance and a spring in my step. I was all in.

Coach Kelican asked me if I would go to a summer football camp, as he knew I went to camps every summer and he wanted to get a group of guys together to go. We got about 30 guys together and went to camp for a week. Through my focus and mindset, I won back a starting position, this time on the defensive line.

As basketball season approached, I did double workouts every day: football practice in the afternoon and running sprints and suicides and shooting baskets at the gym in the evenings. My senior year was coming up, and I knew I had to be all in if I wanted to succeed at basketball.

I was not initially in the starting lineup on the varsity team in my senior year but was the sixth man. I was okay with that, as my favorite player was John Havlicek, a fellow Ohioan and sixth man for the Celtics. I knew the sixth man played almost as much, if not more, than the starters. The season started strong, and I was having a lot of playing time and contributing.

When we began district play, we were going against a team with the number one college recruit in the state of Virginia. He averaged over 25 points a game and was 6 feet 5 inches. At practice before that Friday night game, Coach Hambleton gave us the scouting report and asked if anyone thought they could stop the top recruit. I raised my hand, and he and the assistant coach, Coach Sullivan, started to chuckle. That made me more determined than ever.

"What makes you think you can guard the best player in the state?" Coach Sullivan asked.

"Give me a chance, and I'll show you," I said.

What he didn't know was what happened a few years prior when I was at the basketball camp at the University of Cincinnati with Oscar Robertson. Robertson had told me to focus on my defense and I would always get playing time, as no one wants to play defense. That is why I spent as much time on defense and rebounding as I did on my offensive skills.

Coach Sullivan put me through the wringer during practice. I was tired at the end of practice but determined. That evening, I went home and called Coach Rogers in Martinsburg to get some pointers. Coach Rogers told me to believe in myself, and to focus on defense and not worry about scoring. He encouraged me to show the coaches that I could do the job and back up actions with results.

That Friday night, I kept the number one college recruit to 10 points while I scored 20. I didn't tell the coaches, "I told you so," but in my mind I did. That experience showed me that if I stayed focused, I could accomplish anything.

Those lessons from my mother and Coach Rogers not only served me in high school, but also gave me a great lesson that would help me in the most critical times throughout my life. I didn't get an athletic scholarship to college, which I'd hoped for, but I had learned a much more valuable lesson.

In early 1992, I was coming off a great year in sales. I was the top salesperson in my office and one of the top in the region. I wasn't cocky, but I was very confident. When I got back from the President's Club meeting in San Diego, California, I got a little lazy. I was still selling consistently, but I didn't have the drive that I had the previous couple years.

I spent a lot of time playing golf with my clients, who were bankers and CPAs in South Carolina, as a way to prospect. I thought this would set me up for another stellar year. But by October of that year, I hadn't won an office sales contest in the past few months and I was getting a little frustrated.

I hadn't spoken to Bill since before I went to the President's Club in August, so I called him and suggested we get together. I needed some wisdom and knew that Bill would give me some inspiration. Bill met me for dinner at Beef and Bottle, the restaurant where I had taken my wife for our first date, and he paid for our dinner.

I shared what had been going on with work the past several months, and Bill could sense my anxiety. Over our steak dinners he shared something that happened to him early in his career.

"I had just opened up my second theater, and I was on a roll," Bill said. "Things were going well; people wanted to go to the movies, and I had the formula to grow my business."

Bill's goal was to open five theaters around Charlotte and in South Carolina in his third year. He got the money from his investors and started to open the theaters, but the first and second theaters began to lose money. He went back to fix the problems at those theaters, and the newer ones started to struggle. He told me that he was busier than he had ever been, but he wasn't making any progress.

"I felt like I was in quicksand," Bill said. "I met with my mentor to get my mind right. He told me a couple of things that put me back on track."

First, he told Bill that if he was going to be truly wealthy, not just financially but in every aspect of his life, he needed specialized knowledge in his craft and he had to stay focused. Second, and more importantly, Bill's mentor said, "Activity does not equal accomplishment." He told Bill to focus on the basics and the results he wanted, not the busywork.

Bill told me that those two lessons helped him always stay focused on the results he wanted and not get distracted by things that wouldn't serve his bigger mission of providing a place where people could go to have a wholesome family experience.

That next day, I set new goals. I turned my focus to being the number one salesperson who served his clients better than anyone in the Charlotte office. I went back to the basics. Later that year, I not only became the salesperson of the year for our Charlotte office, but also made the President's Club and the Board of Directors for President's Club.

I used the same game plan I had learned from my mom and Coach Rogers during my senior year in high school, which was reinforced by Bill. Stay focused and put your nose to the grindstone. With that philosophy I knew I could accomplish anything I put my mind to.

Shortly after the Miracle on the Hudson, I was asked during an interview for a German magazine, "If you could have any superpower, what would it be?" I replied, "The ability to focus immediately on the outcome at hand." That day on the airplane, I learned in a way I had not experienced before just how important focus was to my survival.

I heard the explosion on the plane. I had never heard anything like that before, and it got my attention. I looked up and saw fire coming out from underneath the left wing of the Airbus 320. I still wasn't panicked, but I went into a state of awareness. It wasn't until we started to cross over the George Washington Bridge, and we heard, "This is your captain. Brace for impact," that I began to put two and two together.

I had to have laser focus in that situation to keep my mind attuned to the actions necessary for survival. I knew I couldn't let the outside noises and other external factors serve as a distraction.

Many things in life had given me the skills to focus on that situation, starting with sports as a young student athlete. There were things in my career that helped hone those skills as well. In 1997, I was excited to start work on the security team for Tony Robbins. It was a volunteer position, but it was a coveted position. One of the greatest benefits was the ability to see and hear the content Tony was going to present at his events before he went onstage.

I remember at his Life Mastery event in Kona, Hawaii, one of the seminars was focused on mastering your time. I have always been fascinated by how the best of the best manage their time. I knew from experience that people who are successful leave clues to their success, clues you can find if you're alert and watching, so I was always watching and learning from Tony.

I was backstage before he went on and saw for the first time his Outcome Purpose Action (OPA) time management strategy. As he presented the content, I have to admit that I was more a participant than a security team member. I was mesmerized as he laid out the strategy, and I took copious notes. I bought his OPA system at the event and started to use it.

I got the gist of how to implement it, but probably didn't utilize it in the most effective manner. It wasn't until I got an opportunity for one-on-one mentoring with Tony that I really maximized this strategy. I learned that if I focused on the outcome and did only the actions needed to achieve it, I would not only save time but make massive strides toward my goals.

On January 15, 2009, the OPA strategy I learned from Tony played a part in saving my life and helping others on that plane. I had to truly focus as we crossed the George Washington Bridge. I had less than two minutes to "get my mind right," as my dad would say. I knew what outcome I wanted, I knew my purpose, and now it was time to put that game plan together and execute. Fortunately, I had several people and references in my past that gave me the game plan on how to focus and have some control over my destiny.

After we crashed and I survived the impact, I had to stay focused. The disaster was only beginning as the water rapidly entered the plane. I had a game plan and went into focused execution mode. This is a process I'd used many times in the past. For example, if I was late for a plane, I would focus on making a safe drive to the airport without missing any turns and getting through security without distractions. I would tell myself, "Execute, execute, execute," to keep my brain focused on the task at hand.

That day on the Hudson River, with freezing-cold water flooding into the plane, I said to myself, "Execute, execute, execute." This time the stakes were much higher than making a touchdown or getting to my boarding gate on time. I was in a life-or-death situation. People around me were panicking, the situation was changing from one moment to the next, and I started hearing my mother's voice in my head. But with all of that going on, I stayed in that focused state.

For the next eight minutes, I used that superpower of focusing on the outcome at hand to get to safety. That day turned from a potential tragedy to a miracle for me. By staying focused, that miracle, that significant event, helped me find my purpose.

I had learned from Bill that activity does not equal accomplishment. At the time, I took his advice to change my course of action in my career: rather than spinning my wheels by doing a lot of actions that weren't resulting in sales, I honed my goals and focused in on my work. That day on the Hudson River showed me another facet to that lesson. Accomplishments, success in life, and miracles happen when you stay focused on the mission at hand. As Napoleon Hill wrote in *Think and Grow Rich*, "Focus on the possibilities for success, not on the potential for failure," and you, too, can create miracles every day.

Putting It into Practice

Always remember that your focus determines your reality. Throughout my life, when I lost focus on what was necessary to reach my goals, that was the moment I got off track. When I had some adversity and started a pity party for myself, I lost focus on the bigger picture and began down a road that didn't go where I wanted. When I began to focus on having too good a time, my grades would suffer, or my sales numbers would plummet. If I hadn't stayed focused during those critical moments on US Airways Flight 1549, I might not even be here today. Keeping your mind right and focused can turn your challenges into miracles.

Create an Action Plan

Tony Robbins's OPA strategy, to create an Outcome-focused, Purpose-driven Action plan, is helpful in honing your focus.

It took years for me to get to that point in my own life. I worked on Tony's security team for more than 10 years. Every time I would pick him up and transport him, he would ask, "Dave, are you working for yourself yet? Why are you still working for somebody else? Work for yourself. You can make it!"

I kept telling him, "I'm not ready yet." I thought I needed to make more money first. Or I had to get my kids into college. I always had reasons, but those were just excuses, and Tony doesn't deal with excuses very well. I finally realized that he was right. I needed to quit working for other people.

The first thing I did was implement Tony's time management approach: Outcome, Purpose, Action (OPA) strategy. OPA gives you focus. It helps you stay focused on the outcomes you are driving for. Once you learn it, you learn to do only the actions necessary to get the result, not all the activities you think you need to do. It keeps you on the right track.

Once I implemented an OPA strategy, I had the blueprint for making the move I knew was my destiny. It took me a few years to do the activities I needed to do, but ultimately, on February 1, 2014, I made the move to start my own business and live my mission. Every week, I put together my weekly OPA plan. Every day, I start my day by doing my OPA plan for the day. It helps me stay focused on what is truly important in my life and my mission.

Resist Distractions

Even after you create an action plan to help you reach your goals, life will throw distractions your way. Work to find the best way to avoid those distractions. For me, having the mantra of "execute, execute, execute" serves to keep me focused on the task at hand. Maybe you can find help focusing by practicing meditation techniques. It could be as simple as turning off the notifications on your email and phone to allow you uninterrupted time to work.

When I look back on that day on the Hudson River, I can see that I had an OPA plan in my head. I knew the outcome I wanted: to stay alive. I knew the purpose: I wanted to be around for my children and their lives. With that in my head, I focused on the actions I needed to do to get off the sinking plane.

Remember to focus on taking massive action and the triumph will follow. Accomplishments, not actions, and you, too, can have your date with destiny!

This is the game in which my coaches gave me the start position against the top recruit in the state of Virginia. I'm going in for a layup wrong footed!

Lesson Eight: Persistence Pays Dividends

Summer 1966

My parents joined the Highland Swim Club for two reasons. First, they wanted to make sure my sister and I learned to swim, and second, they wanted to give us someplace to go while school was out, as my mom was pregnant with our brother.

I was five years old, and swimming didn't come easily for me. I liked going to the pool to play, but I really didn't want to take lessons early in the morning. I fought it but my mother persisted. When I would get frustrated after a lesson and ask to quit, she told me to keep trying.

She knew how to reward me. She told me that once I learned how to swim, first I could go to the pool by myself, and then I could go to the pool with friends. She started early in my life with positive reinforcement to get me to keep trying.

That summer I learned how to swim and was very proud of myself, but that wasn't the end of it for my mother, who wanted me to keep trying. Each summer I went for additional swimming badges, until finally she pushed me toward getting lifeguard certification. Once again, I pushed back on her.

"I already know how to swim, so why do I need to get my lifeguard certification?"

"Knowing how to swim is one aspect. Getting that certification will open many more opportunities for you," she said.

Of course, I did what my mom wanted and started working on my certification. I got to the final test and saw what I had to do.

It was overwhelming! Not only was I required to be able to swim 500 yards nonstop, but I also had to know first aid, how to handle emergencies, how to remove people from the pool who were bigger than me, and how to use other items, such as backboards and rings, to rescue people. I told my mom that I couldn't do all that. My mother gave me the response that she gave me other times I told her I couldn't do something: "There is no such word as can't!"

In 1971, you could only fail the requirements two times before you had to start over. After I failed the first time, I didn't have a lot of confidence that I could pass the second time and didn't want to start over and retake the course. That became my excuse, but my mom kept telling me, "Keep trying. There is no such word as can't!" I went for it again. I passed the first aid and the exercise of pulling someone out of the pool. Now I had to get through my nemesis, the 500-yard swim. The Red Cross trainer told me to pace myself; there was no time limit.

My mindset when I was 11 was to get through whatever I was doing as quickly as possible, so pacing myself was a challenge. I only wanted it to be over, but I took his advice, slowed down, and took my time. I don't remember how long it took me to finish, but I did it, and my mom was at the end of the pool when I got done. I swam 500 yards without stopping, and I finally passed! I didn't have to retake the course, and best of all, when I turned 12, I could be a junior lifeguard!

My mom hugged me and took me to the Dairy Queen to celebrate. My mom was smart. By pushing me to finish that course and get certified, she anchored in me one more time that if I persisted and succeeded, I could accomplish anything.

At the same time that I was going for my lifeguard certification, I was working hard in Boy Scouts. I was working on my path to Eagle, but I also wanted to get the Order of the Arrow (OA) and be an Arrow man. To be able to go for the Order of the Arrow honor, you need to have 15 nights of camping and be a First-Class Scout. I met these requirements.

My scoutmaster, Lawson Walker, nominated me to go for the OA honor. I signed up for the first OA certification in the spring of 1972. It was about this time that my father told us we would be moving to Virginia, so I knew I had to get it done before we moved.

My dad dropped me off at the state camp in Delaware, Ohio, on a Friday for the Order of the Arrow weekend. I didn't know a single soul at that camp. Dad said he'd see me on Sunday, and he left. It was the first time I was left alone without any friends around. It was a little intimidating, but I knew there were other boys about my age in the same situation.

When I checked in, the scoutmaster gave me a log and instructions. I liken it to Survivor on steroids, as we had to do several activities throughout the weekend with little sleep. On Saturday night, we had to prove we had completed all the activities and then present the whittled log in the shape of an arrow. Once I had my instructions, off I went into the woods with a group of boys I didn't know.

Friday evening was tough. There were stations all around the camp to test us on tying knots, building a fire, building a little shed from logs, teamwork, and many other skills. At first our group wanted to stop and sleep for a while, but with all the things we had to do, we decided to keep going through the night. We finally stopped at 3:00 a.m., but we had to get back up at 5:00 a.m., as we only had until 5:00 p.m. Saturday to finish all the activities in addition to whittling the log down.

It was a pace I wasn't used to keeping. Early Saturday morning, after we ate, we had to get to the next activity, which was across a river which cut through the camp. We looked at the river, and then we noticed a bridge about a half mile downriver. We discussed walking to the bridge and crossing, but that would take a lot of time, so we decided we would swim across the river to save time.

When we made that decision, I was truly glad that my mom had kept after me to get my lifeguard certification. I knew I could swim across the river, even with my backpack and log, as I had to do something similar in my lifeguard test with the backboards and rings we had to carry. We all got across the river, but we were all tired.

I started to think, "Is this all worth it?"

I kept hearing my mom in my head telling me to keep trying. At the end of the day, we had completed all the activities and made our way back to the lodge. Now all I had to do was present my wooden arrow at that evening's installation. I kept working on my arrow up until it was time to get dressed for the event. That evening, I presented my list of activities and my arrow to the scoutmaster.

I received my Order of the Arrow honor and became a lifelong member of the Order. If my mom hadn't pushed me to learn to swim and get my junior lifeguard certification, I might have never been able to get this honor. She probably never knew that that first swimming lesson when I was five would serve me many more times.

Right before my family moved to Virginia, my father bought an organ. I didn't know why, but both my parents insisted that my sister and I learn how to play. I liked playing the drums, but when we got to Virginia, they made us take organ lessons. I was more focused on playing sports and making new friends, and I fought my parents on learning how to play. When I had lessons, I would not put any effort into it. I didn't practice; I couldn't play the chords.

One night at dinner, my father exploded and told me I was going to learn how to play the organ, and that was that. I never knew why he was so adamant about me learning how to play the organ, but I knew if I was going to get to keep doing the things I loved—sports and Scouts—I would have to do this too.

I didn't like the music the instructor kept giving me to learn, and I think that is why I kept pushing back. For Christmas in 1974, my parents gave me my first record player and album. It was a K-Tel album with a lot of hits and songs from many different artists. I would listen to that album over and over, and I bet my dad was ready to throw it out the window, but as I listened, I heard a couple of songs that had the organ or keyboard in the arrangement.

My dad had this huge sound system in the family room where the organ was. One day, I brought that K-Tel album down to the family room, queued it up for the Deep Purple song *Smoke on the Water,* and started to play along with the song. My mom came in and asked me what I was doing. I told her I was practicing the organ. I totally butchered the song, but I was playing. The next day I did the same thing, but this time I put on the song from The Doors, *Break On Through (To the Other Side).*

As I played along with the band, I started to get the hang of playing rock music on the organ. I kept trying and persisted until I could play along with the song. I couldn't play Beethoven, but I could play The Doors. My parents and I learned a valuable lesson through that. Getting me to practice the organ took finding the music that I liked and giving me a reason to play that made sense to me. Just like with swimming lessons, I needed the right motivation to make me practice. Again, I showed that with the right motivation, I could persist until I succeeded.

The lesson that persistence pays off served me well during my years working with Howard Johnson. It was my first job out of college, and I wanted to make a good impression. I kept my head down and worked hard to improve and stand out.

That paid off when I was given the promotion to first assistant restaurant manager. That would mean moving away from Charlotte, so I consulted Bill about what to do. He told me that if I wanted to grow with the company, I would have to be flexible. I would get a significant increase in pay, and Howard Johnson would give me one weekend off a month so I could go back to see Terri, and I decided to take it.

That promotion took me to Wytheville, Virginia. I worked with a manager I knew, and that store was one of the top 10 revenue stores in the company, so bonuses were in play now. I was on the fast track to having my own store. For the next year, I was focused on growing with the company. I wanted to get the promotion to store manager.

Terri had a great job at Pic 'n Pay and was advancing in her job as well, but we still found time to see each other, driving back and forth between Wytheville and Charlotte.

After 11 months, the district manager visited me in Wytheville and told me he wanted to move me to my hometown of Winchester. I thought he was going to offer me a store manager position, but there was no Howard Johnson in Winchester. He told me that the company had sold several stores to Marriott, and Winchester was one of those stores. He wanted me to be the first assistant and train to open new stores or convert existing Howard Johnson stores to Bob's Big Boy.

I knew I was in a dead-end position with Howard Johnson, and if I wanted to get promoted, I probably needed to make a move. Before I called Terri, I called Bill and arranged to come to Charlotte to meet him the next day, as I needed to let the district manager know my decision by that Monday.

I laid out the scenario for Bill and told him I was confused. I wanted to take the opportunity, but I also had to think about Terri.

"Did I ever tell you about the decision I had to make in 1963?" Bill asked. "At the time I had about 15 theaters in the Charlotte area. Things were going well, and I was approached with an offer to buy me out. If I sold out, Bonnie and I could live the rest of our lives comfortably, but the contract stated I couldn't buy or open any other theaters in the area for five years. If I didn't sell, I'd have to keep working hard to keep growing."

At the time, there was a lot going on in the world. There was civil unrest in the South, and the Vietnam War was getting hot. "That unrest in Vietnam brought back memories about Korea and our son. It was difficult for me to keep going, and the offer to sell out looked pretty good, but there was just something about it that didn't seem right," Bill said.

Bill called his mentor for advice. He told Bill something that not only helped him make that decision, but also drove him toward even more success. His mentor said, "If you believe in your mission, you must persevere. You cannot let anyone else determine your destiny but you."

Bill rejected the investor's offer and started to expand his theaters and other real estate ventures. The late 1960s and early 1970s were a time when Bill not only made most of his money, but he also helped others open restaurants and theaters. If he had sold out, his and Bonnie's lives might not have been what they were, and those others he helped may never have seen their dreams come true.

As far as my promotion, he told me to make a decision and not look back. He recommended that I take the promotion and move, as Marriott was a big company, and I may be able to get Terri a job in Northern Virginia.

I took Terri out to dinner that evening and discussed the move, and she supported me. We both had to make some sacrifices, but we knew this was an opportunity I couldn't pass up. I accepted the promotion on Monday and by the next weekend, was back in Winchester.

Terri came up once a month, and I went to Charlotte once a month. I learned, as I did when I was young, that if I persevered and persisted in getting what I was going for, I could determine my destiny. No one else could. When you persevere, you can "break on through to the other side."

That lesson was foundational in my life, especially on January 15, 2009.

The plane had crashed into the river. Water was streaming into the Airbus 320. When I got to the door at 10F, I looked out and saw a problem. There was no room on that wing for me. There was no room in that lifeboat for me. I was halfway out of US Airways Flight 1549. I was waist deep in 36° water and had been for over seven minutes. I was stuck in the doorway, waiting for something to open up so I could make my move.

If you have ever been stuck in a doorway, you know it is an uncomfortable position to be in. You are in a state of uncertainty. Should I continue forward, or should I retreat to perceived safety? It is a threshold moment—a PITTChE. Something is going to happen, and what you choose will change your life. This is a moment in your life that genuinely matters.

I felt the plane shift. I found out later that a tugboat had hit the front of the sinking plane as it was backing out. Once I felt that shift, the first thing I thought was "Titanic!" I knew the plane was going down, and it was now or never. I made the decision to jump into the 36° Hudson River and swim to the closest boat I could find.

I've thought about that moment many times since. It reminded me of the time I was going for my Order of the Arrow honor. That day, I jumped into a river with my clothes and backpack on and swam to the other side. I was a little afraid, but I did it. I persevered.

In the doorway of that plane, when it came time to make my move, I had a strong reference to look back on that helped me know I could do it. I had the certainty that if I did it once, I could do it again, even in 36° water. That was the longest 10-yard swim in my life. I got to the ferry at the end of the right wing and held on to the hanging ladder.

People were yelling at me to climb up. I yelled up, "I can't!" But then I heard my mom's voice saying, "There is no such word as can't!" She would never let me say those words. I got one arm up and felt someone grab it. I got the other arm up and felt someone grab it. They pulled me up to the ferry and hauled me over the edge.

I survived a plane crash and a sinking plane. Even though I wasn't out of the woods yet, the lessons I learned about never giving up got me through. I learned to persist until I got my desired outcome. It was a lesson that saved my life.

Putting It into Practice

Your success throughout your life starts with a dream. Perseverance is an essential quality if you want to accomplish your outcomes and achieve success.

Develop a Habit of Perseverance through Faith

First, it helps to understand perseverance. Perseverance is persisting in moving forward despite challenges and disappointments. When you are armed with perseverance, your success in obtaining the things you want in life—business success, personal fulfillment, passionate relationships—is almost guaranteed.

Once you decide what you want, you need faith that you can accomplish it. Your faith will give you the momentum and motivation to continually go after your dream and desired outcomes, regardless of challenges you come up against.

Possessing a deep inner faith that you can succeed means that you will never give up on your dreams. You will have the mindset that you can accomplish anything. You will encounter significant challenges, but because you have faith that you will eventually succeed, you will be able to modify and change your plan of action and tweak your strategies to keep advancing and dramatically improve your chances of success.

Set a Timeline

Commit yourself to a timeline for reaching your goals, to give you a specific time to work toward. Do not quit before that date! The key to perseverance is remembering my mother's words, "There is no such word as can't." When you quit, it only inhibits your ability to persevere.

Find Family and Friends for a Support Network

Having people around you for support helps keep you focused. We all stumble from time to time. If you hit a roadblock or need support in your life, it helps to have people who will encourage you to persevere and persist and help you reach your outcome.

In the end, our perseverance is rewarded throughout our lives. Reaching the final goal and finding fulfillment makes the temporary suffering seem insignificant in comparison.

THE AMERI ONAL RED CROSS

SWIMMER

This certifies that
David Sanderson
is qualified as an
ADVANCED BEGINNER IN SWIMMING
having passed the required tests at
Highland Co. Swim Club

8/31/71
Date Course Completed

R.M Oswald
National Director
Safety Programs

My mom would not let me give up when I had to swim the five hundred yards to get my Advanced Beginner Badge, which led to becoming a junior lifeguard. She was very proud when I did it. It became even more poignant on January 15, 2009.

Lesson Nine: Take Action to Meet Your Goals

December 16, 1976

It was the night of an away game for my junior high basketball team. I was at a school where junior high was seventh grade through ninth grade, and as a ninth grader, I was really hitting my stride. I excelled not only in the classroom but also in athletics. The coaches noticed and let me work out with the high school teams. It was a way to give me the ability to really hit the ground running once I got to high school, to have not only a better chance at making the varsity teams, but also to get some real playing time.

I'd made friends with some of the high school athletes, and they came with our team to one of our games to support us, riding the team bus as well. It was the protocol that if your parents came to a game, you were allowed to ride home with them, not having to ride the team bus back to the school, but this time I wanted to ride with my team, to hang out with the high school kids who had come to watch me play. I told my parents that I would be riding the bus. I thought I was doing what my mom had taught me—to take action.

One of the first lessons I remember her sharing with me was about taking action. I learned that action is a necessary part of all our relationships—with our family, teachers, friends, and your Creator.

I learned early in my life that my "inner demons" or those who may have a different agenda than I, our enemies take advantage of those who choose passivity over action. Action requires faith and trust in those who are in our lives. Mom told me that the fearful and the doubters will always struggle to act. She told me that I could have an advantage in life by staying busy and taking action. With her help, I learned at a very young age that if I stayed busy, had faith, and was focused, I could accomplish almost anything I wanted.

Apparently, getting on that bus wasn't the type of action my mom had been teaching me about. A few minutes after I boarded, my mom walked down that aisle, grabbed me by the ear, and took me off the bus. Our house was about 10 miles from the school, and she was not going to go out of her way to pick me up when I could ride home with them.

It was a humbling and confusing time for me. Humbling because my mom physically took me off the bus in front of my friends, and confusing because I thought I was doing what I'd been taught—to take action to get what I wanted. This time I took action and was humiliated. Something didn't jive.

It seemed to me that my growing up years were full of times when I was figuring out what exactly my mom meant when she told me to take action for myself.

That bus incident gave me a bad taste in my mouth for riding the bus. After being humiliated once, I didn't feel much like getting back on the bus with my peers. Therefore, when I got to high school, I did all I could to find a way to avoid riding the bus.

I thought my older sister would be my ride, but that turned out not to be the case. She and I ran with different crowds, and she drove her friends and "didn't have room" for me. We also had different activities, so she didn't have time to drive me to school and run me to all my practices.

During the summer at football camp, I'd made friends with some of the upperclassmen. When it came time for school to begin, I approached my football teammates to drive me to school, but none of them lived close to me. So, I ended up taking the bus.

Riding the bus inspired me to take my mom's advice again and act. I had to get resourceful. I ultimately found a friend to drive me to school, but I still needed a ride home after practice. Occasionally, I had teammates who would drive me home, but they were not reliable.

In 1976, there was no such thing as mobile phones, so my mom gave me a dime every day to call her from the pay phone when I needed a ride. The dime would become a metaphor for action for me during my high school years.

After home games, the team would go out to Pizza Hut or have parties if we won. My parents wanted me to enjoy these times, but they had a hard and fast rule: curfew was 11:00 p.m. sharp. Since the games weren't over until around 9:30 and we didn't get out of the locker room until after 10:00, that didn't leave much time to hang out. Getting home by 11:00 was tough. The excuse that I didn't have anyone to bring me home didn't work. My mother told me that there was always a phone available, and I had a dime. Her mindset was, "There is no excuse not to call."

More often than not, I didn't take her advice and ended up grounded. But ultimately, I learned the lesson my mother was trying to teach me. My mindset and my personal demons would take advantage of me if I chose passivity instead of action. I could have an advantage by staying focused and taking action.

In 1999, I had just made a move to KPMG and was a part of their first sales team. After being with PeopleSoft, I thought making a move to consulting would broaden my skill set and make me more marketable. Traditionally, Big Five accounting firms had partners doing sales and service. KPMG was on the cutting edge by bringing in seasoned sales representatives to find and develop opportunities.

My strategy whenever I made a move to a new sales position was to make a big splash by getting a sale quickly. When I began with KPMG, I had the same game plan. After training, I jumped in and started to prospect in the consumer industrial market. At the beginning, I struggled. I had thought the sales role at KPMG would be similar to my roles at the other companies I sold for, but it turned out to be different.

One of the first companies I approached was one of the largest beverage companies in the world. I had found an opportunity for a strategy project. I was stoked and brought it back to my partner in Atlanta, Georgia. We discussed it, and I introduced him to the team at the beverage company.

After the meeting, we debriefed, and he thanked me and told me that he would take the reins now. I was a part of the team, but he and his managers would run the opportunity. I was disappointed and discussed this with my manager. Since this role was not only new for the sales team but also for the partners, the partners wanted their sales teams to just "bird dog" the opportunities and not sell; selling was the partners' responsibility. My manager said that if the company made the sale, I would get paid.

As the opportunity started to develop, I could see that we were not positioned very well. I kept telling the KPMG partner on this pursuit and his managers that we needed to create other relationships and find a coach. The partner had his methodology, but I could see that it wasn't the right approach. I was frustrated and started questioning my move to KPMG.

When it was time for my traditional holiday lunch with Bill, I was champing at the bit to tell him what was going on and get his advice. I didn't know it would be our last holiday lunch meeting, which in hindsight, makes it even more special.

I shared with Bill what was going on at KPMG. I was told I was doing well, but I felt like a high-priced prospector. Bill shared with me a time when he learned a lesson that helped him change the direction in his own business.

When Germany entered Poland on September 1, 1939, war rumblings were starting in the United States. The Americans weren't in the war yet, but American factories started production and began to supply England and its armed services. The economy was coming back after the Great Depression.

For Bill's theater business, that news was both good and bad.

"The jobs meant people had more disposable income, which meant they could afford to go to the movies," Bill said. "But on the other hand, they were working more and had less free time to go to the theater."

It was a time when even Hollywood was booming, and lots of great films were coming out, but Bill and his management teams struggled to get people to come to their theaters.

"I met with my mentor to discuss the situation with him. He said to remember that my employees were a reflection of my own leadership," Bill said. "When I acted deflated and uninspired, so would my management team and all our employees. My mentor said, 'It sounds like you're waiting for a roasted chicken to jump in your mouth!'"

That's when Bill had an epiphany. He couldn't just wait around for things to happen as they had in the past; he had to put a plan together and take action. He had to find something to inspire his team and get people excited to come to the movies again.

Hollywood gave Bill the perfect opportunity, as 1939 was when color started coming into films. What could Bill do in his theaters to reflect this new way to see a movie? Was he advertising in the newspapers? Through the Depression years Bill had done okay with a passive business model, but now he had to change the game to get the attention of people who had alternatives to going to the movies.

Bill learned that being passive was an enemy to his business. He and his team found some ways to act. He invested in new equipment to show these new color movies in the best way possible. Then he put color into everything he did, including advertising, so when people thought of going out to the movies, they would think of his theaters. His business started to grow and expand.

On December 7, 1941, things changed again. Now the US was involved in World War II. Bill used the same strategy: taking action. He shifted to showing war movies that focused on supporting the United States.

Those stories inspired me. I learned from Bill that I needed to get busy, take action, and change the game I was playing.

The next week, I went to Atlanta without any of my colleagues from KPMG to meet with my point of contact at my prospective new beverage client. I learned a few things and found out why we were behind in the pursuit. We could have all the functional capabilities they needed, but we would never get through if our team didn't understand and address the prospect's company culture.

I got back to Charlotte and arranged a call with the pursuit team. It turns out that they had news for me as well. They said our beverage prospect's most prominent rival was an audit client for KPMG. Due to a noncompete clause, if we were going to go for this new business, KPMG would have to recuse itself from the audit. I thought, at this point did it even make sense to bring up what I'd learned if we couldn't pursue the opportunity? But I remembered the lesson I had learned from Bill: I needed to take action if I was going to change the game.

Our opportunity was four times bigger than the annual audit revenue. But the audit client was a sure thing, whereas the beverage company wasn't at that point. Was it worth the risk to give up the current revenue for the chance we might not even get the prospect as a client? I remembered my mom's advice: "You always have a dime." I decided to go for it.

I told the team that if we could find a former employee who could give us guidance and information of the inner workings about the beverage company culture, we could not only get back in the game but also could win. At first the team thought I was "out to lunch", but I asked them to let me try to find someone.

I asked my partner to go to the managing partner for the beverage company's competitor and start to open up the possibility of giving up the audit. It was a high-risk move. I knew I could lose my job if we lost a client and didn't win the prospective client.

I spent the next week looking for a former employee from the prospective client. These were the days before LinkedIn. I spent hours on the phone. I took massive action, got resourceful, and used my network. Finally, I found a retired attorney who had worked there. I spoke with him, and he was open to helping us, but he was a consultant and consultants cost money. This time my action wasn't a dime, it was $10,000!

I went back to my team and told them about this gentleman. I introduced him to the team, and the partner made the call to go for it. We paid our consultant his fee and went all in. KPMG subsequently gave up the audit for the competitor, and we won a $5-million project. By staying focused, taking action, and changing the game, I made my mark at KPMG, which set me on my path to bigger and better opportunities.

Flash forward to 2009. US Airways Flight 1549 was filling with water. We survived the crash, but now we had a bigger problem. Was the plane going to sink before we could get off it? The final thought I had before impact was "aisle, up, out." I knew if I survived the crash, I had to take action and do it quickly. I looked up toward the aisle and saw people not only walking down the aisle waist-deep in water, but also walking down the seats on each side of the plane.

When it was my time to go, I got to the aisle and my plan was to go up and out. But at that moment, I heard my mom's voice in my head: "If you do the right thing, God will take care of you!" I knew at that moment that I had to take action. I could have gone up the aisle, but I looked around and saw so many people still in the plane. I'd grown up with the motto "Never Leave Anyone Behind."

I took action, climbing over the seats to the back of the plane to see if anyone needed help. The water was chest-deep in the back of the aircraft, but people were moving. I got behind the last person and watched to see if anyone needed help. Luggage floated in the water from the bins that had opened on impact and from under the seats. It was getting dark inside the plane, as it was late in the day in January.

I made my way up, and when I saw the light from the door on the right, I thought, "I'm out of here." When I got to the door at 10F, I looked out and saw the ferries. People who had already gotten out of the sinking plane were being rescued.

If myself and others didn't take massive action on January 15, 2009, we all might not be here today. What I learned as a youth and throughout my life served me well that day. Choosing action over passivity kept my internal "demons" at bay, or in this instance, kept us alive. Action requires faith and trust that you can and will succeed in any area of your life.

Putting It into Practice

My mentors throughout the years all passed along the importance of taking action, but what exactly does that look like? As I learned when I was a kid, sometimes taking action can backfire, but did that keep me from taking action again? No.

Use those times as a learning experience. If I learned anything from my mentors over the years, whether it was my parents, Bill, or Tony Robbins, it's that it is important to take massive action in every aspect of your life.

Change Your To-Do List to Your Action Plan

During my time working as security director for Tony Robbins, I had the opportunity to go with him when he spoke to a professional sports team. When you have a room full of millionaire athletes, sometimes it's hard to get their attention. Tony is the master and quickly got them to listen. This team was on a losing streak, and he was brought in to share why winners win and losers lose.

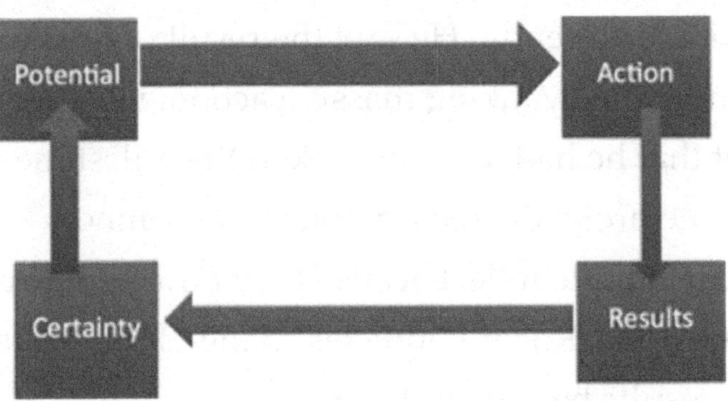

He showed them his model for success and how it starts with potential, but without action that potential goes nowhere. It takes action to get a result. That result could be positive or negative, win or lose. Once you get the result, you get a belief, positive or negative, from that result.

Now that you have a belief, the cycle starts again—only now you have more potential to act and get a result and gain more beliefs. Tony used the Chicago Bulls as an example. In the 1990s, the Bulls had a lot of potential. Their team took action, got positive results, and that led to a strong belief that they were winners. That gave them even more potential, and the cycle sped up. They won six NBA championships.

Contrast that with Roger Bannister, the first man to break the four-minute mile. How did he break the mark that no one had come close to in previously recorded history? Bannister used the same success model the Bulls used, but he did one thing differently. He saw the result of breaking the four-minute mile by taking massive action, which gave him the belief that he had already broken the milestone. The year after he broke the record, four more runners achieved a four-minute mile, because they now had a belief that it could be done. Roger Bannister changed the game by seeing the results before he started.

Bannister and the Bulls of the '90s didn't just have a to-do list that included winning games and breaking world records. They made their goals an action plan.

By changing the game from a list of tasks to accomplish into an action plan for success, you give yourself the belief that you can get the result you are after before you even start!

Don't Confuse Listening with Passivity

One thing I learned, first from my mother, then from my mentors, Bill and Tony Robbins, is the importance of taking action in every aspect of your life. Sometimes that means listening to others and paying attention to what's going on in the world around you. Many of us struggle with fully and attentively listening to what other people are trying to teach us. Most of us tend to speak brashly, spouting our opinions before we've either heard a person out or listened to the small voice in our heads.

The discipline of listening can be misunderstood as passivity; however, those who've learned to act with quietness have the significant advantage of wisdom and insight.

As I speak with those few people who have found success and fulfillment, I find they understand that taking action takes many forms. Listening is just as important as speaking. It helps you make sure the actions you take will lead to the results you want.

Onstage at my TEDx Talk at Queens University in Kingston, Ontario. I set my mind on bringing something new and innovative to a TEDx Talk, something the audience and event staff had never seen before. I incorporated visual scribe technology into my presentation.

Lesson Ten:
Tools for Decision-Making

March 31, 1967

I was six years old, sitting at the table in my grandmother's kitchen. One of the things I cherish most about my youth is the times I spent in Illinois with my grandmother. On those visits, she and I had what she called our "kitchen summits." We would talk, and she'd tell me stories about her family. It was during one of those summits on this particular visit that she said something I would hear again later in life.

"What do you do, Grandma?" I knew she worked at a shoe store, but I didn't know what she did.

"Honey, my job is to teach you grandchildren where the land mines in life are hidden."

At first, I didn't understand what she meant. The only thing I could relate to a land mine was what we saw on TV during the news when Walter Cronkite showed stories about the Vietnam War. I knew what she said was important, so I remembered it for later.

Even at that early age, I knew I could learn a lot from her. She married my grandfather in 1926, and they had seven children together on their farm in Kentucky. Four of those children died, and the Tennessee Valley Authority purchased most of their land, which prompted them to move to Illinois to find a better life and a place to raise my mom and her two sisters. Years of hard work and experiences in life gave my grandmother plenty of stories to share with me.

Every visit, my grandma and I would always have our time in the kitchen talking. I talked to her about everything going on in my life, more than I would say to my parents. She was the one who taught me about loyalty and having someone you could trust without fear of reprisal.

When I told her about something I did wrong, she wouldn't get mad. Instead, she would tell me a story, something that illustrated how later in life I'd have to take responsibility for my decisions and made me aware that I should avoid situations like those that got me in trouble. As far as I know, she never told my parents anything I shared with her, and she taught me always to stay aware and make better decisions.

My grandmother's house is where my cousins and I gathered. We played board games—usually Monopoly and sometimes Risk. If you've never played Risk, the object of the game is to conquer the world. To win, you must attack and defend—attacking to acquire territory and defending to keep your territory from your opponents.

Playing those games with my cousins, I learned how to assess risk and make decisions if I wanted to win. The more decisions I made, the better I got at assessing risks and deciding when and how to take them.

Of course, it wasn't just my grandmother who taught me the benefits of making good decisions. On a daily basis, my parents taught me the importance of making good decisions, and how you have to live with the consequences of your decisions, good or bad.

One time of day when this really came into play was at the dinner table. When I was little, if my mother made something for dinner that I didn't like, I just wouldn't eat it. My father wouldn't get angry, but he gave me a choice to make: eat it or go to bed at 6:30 p.m. Either choice was okay with him, but he always insisted I make the decision for myself. I learned early that there are consequences for every decision you make in your life, good or bad.

The older you get, the more decisions you need to make, and they carry more consequences than going to bed at 6:30. I was fortunate to have teachers and leaders throughout my youth who had a similar set of values as my parents. As I progressed through elementary school, my teachers would hold their students accountable for their actions, and my parents would always back the teachers.

Our house was about a four-mile drive from my school, Washington Elementary, but if we walked out the back of our home and through our lot, there was a path through the woods that got us to the school in about five minutes.

One day in second grade, things weren't going well for me. I had a scuffle on the playground with a classmate. My teacher, Mrs. Stinson, was old-school. She'd let us get our grievances out until it got physical.

This day we were playing marbles during recess, and I thought I had won and should get to take the other boy's marble. This boy and I always got along, so I didn't think anything about it. Fair is fair. He took exception and wouldn't give up the marble. He and I went at it, and punches were thrown, so Mrs. Stinson broke us up and walked us to the principal's office.

In 1967, when we went into the principal's office, the first thing we saw was a paddle with holes in it hanging on the door. Mrs. Stinson left us in the office and went back to the classroom. I knew that if I got paddled at school, things would get even worse at home, so I decided to leave. I cut through the woods and went home to sit in my treehouse until school was over.

I thought I could get out of the paddling, but the principal called my mom. I didn't think my mom knew the shortcut through the woods, but as she walked through the backyard toward the path, she saw me in the treehouse. That day, I learned what my dad had told me about the consequences for my decisions, good or bad.

My mom walked me back to school through the woods, and I had to face the wrath of the principal. I didn't get a paddling there—I just got a stern talking-to—but when I got home from school, I had to sit in the family room until my dad got home. Then discipline was served. I learned at an early age how vital decision-making was going to be in my life.

One of the things taught in Boy Scouts is the skills needed to assess risks and make good choices. My scoutmaster, Lawson Walker, was a big advocate of teaching Scouts these skills. Mr. Walker earned his Eagle Scout in 1919, shortly after World War I ended. He encouraged his Scouts to learn skills through camping and being in the outdoors.

We went camping one weekend every month at the campsite in our region. When I was a First Class Scout, I was responsible for a small group of newer Scouts. During one of these outings, we went to a part of the camp where we could go rock climbing and spelunking. When I was a Tenderfoot and went on these outings, the First Class Scouts would take us out and make the decisions about what we would do. Now that I was a First Class Scout, it was up to me to decide what activities we would do. First up was rock climbing.

I was all in on going rock climbing, but the group was less than enthusiastic. It was my call to go or not to go, but one thing I learned from being around Scoutmaster Walker was that when it came time to make a decision, everyone should have a say; but once everyone had a say, part of leadership was committing to a decision, even with some people disagreeing. Our team discussed it, and I made the call not to climb. It was a difficult decision, but we all committed and moved on to the next activity—spelunking.

I had been spelunking many times. There were many caves around Serpent Mound, a place in southern Ohio where my family would go on short weekend trips. It was an internationally known National Historic Landmark built by the ancient American Indian cultures of Ohio, and my dad took our family there often.

When I was a Tenderfoot Scout, our troop took a trip there, and I was initiated into spelunking. The first time you go spelunking, it can be a little scary. Crawling into a small cave with stalagmites sticking out and water up to your belly is somewhat intimidating. Getting through some of those crevasses was tough, but what was more difficult was working your way out of the caves. I loved exploring, so when we got to that part of the camp, I was stoked to lead my little group through the cave.

Once again, I "took the temperature" of my squad, and there was some trepidation. I decided we would go ahead. It seemed like a good time for me to lead and teach the Tenderfoot Scouts how to face their fear of the dark. It was a great experience, and not only did we all get to share in it, but it also taught me how to lead and make decisions with and for a team. I think this was the first time I worked with a team to make decisions that had risks associated with them.

As I got older, my dad reinforced the importance of decision-making and assessing risk. Two things my dad taught me in order to work through a potentially significant financial decision were:

- You must assess and identify the risk in the decision you are about to make. Is it a reasonable risk or a bad risk to take?
- You must assess and identify the exit strategy for any situation you get into.

The truth is, I didn't understand what he meant by this until I purchased my first car.

I was 22 years old, and I hadn't planned on buying a car that day. I had driven my dad's old Datsun B210 to my job interview in Northern Virginia. It was a basic car with AM radio and no air conditioning, but it had low-cost maintenance and was serviceable. The interview in Tysons Corner went well, and afterward I stopped for lunch. When I got back to my car after lunch, I couldn't get the car started.

"No worries," I thought. "I know how to jump a battery." The manager at the restaurant brought his jumper cables out, but the car wouldn't start. Still no worries—I figured the battery was dead, so I'd get a new battery. I went across the street to the Datsun dealership and asked them to get the car and put a new battery in it.

We got the car to their service station, and while I waited a salesperson came out to talk with me. The service manager came out and told me the car was dead. It didn't need a battery; the engine would need to be serviced or replaced. Now I didn't know what to do. Since the interview had gone well, I decided to take a walk with the salesperson and look at some cars.

I had a friend, Larry Smoot, in Winchester, who had a Datsun 280ZX sports car. I fell in love with that car. As we walked around the lot, I saw a red one. I took a short ride, and the salesperson made an offer I couldn't resist. I could trade in the B210 with no money down and drive the 280ZX home. I made the deal and drove the red 280ZX back home.

When I got home, my dad looked at my new car. He didn't get upset. He asked me to call our State Farm Insurance agent to find out how much the monthly insurance payment would be for it, since I—not my dad—had to pay for the car insurance.

I called Ken, our State Farm agent, and found out it would be $500 a month for auto insurance on a new red Datsun 280ZX. I could afford the car, but I couldn't afford the auto insurance!

My dad asked me how I was going to get out of that purchase. He asked if I had an exit strategy. Of course, I hadn't thought about that. I was happy I had made a big decision and had a sports car! The next day, I returned the Datsun 280ZX, got the B210 started, and drove it to an Oldsmobile dealership where I bought a used 1980 Cutlass Supreme.

Once I thought about all the details that go into making a significant financial decision, I learned a valuable lesson. First, I have to assess all the risks of anything I get into. Second, I need to have an exit strategy on how to get out of a poor decision.

At one of my lunches with Bill, I asked him how he made the big decision to buy his first movie theater. Bill told me that he really wanted to get into the movie industry, and being in North Carolina, the only way he knew he could be a part of things was to buy a movie house. He didn't know anything about business or how to buy anything, but he knew what he wanted. That's when he met the person who would become his mentor.

Bill said that he had to sell his mentor on why and how badly he wanted to own a theater. Once he did that, his mentor started to teach him the mindset he needed to own a business and how to manage and lead his employees.

The first thing he taught Bill was that as a leader, he would make decisions that would not only impact him but also his team.

Bill's mentor told him that when it comes to making these big decisions, procrastination is the worst option. As a leader, you want to make decisions that put you in control of the things happening in your life. When you procrastinate, you lose control. He learned that even when you think you've made the wrong decision, it's better than not making any decision, because you can learn from it. Those lessons will serve you in the most critical of times.

"Making decisions, good or bad, is a crucial attribute to leadership," Bill said.

I told Bill that I was struggling to make decisions in my career. I had a small, growing family, and I didn't want to make a mistake, particularly when it came to financial decisions. Bill reaffirmed that I wouldn't be right 100 percent of the time, but he said that you only have to be right about 51 percent of the time to be successful. He then shared with me the strategy and model that he had learned from his mentor that helped him not only when he decided to invest in his first movie house, but also with subsequent significant decisions.

- **Choose.** The key word in making decisions is to choose. We are the sum total of all the decisions we have made in our lives, plus those times we did not make decisions.
- **Withdraw.** When you need to make a decision, withdraw from the world around you so you can concentrate on the issue at hand.
- **Seek counsel.** One way to do that is to pray. As you make decisions, you should first ask God, and others who have faced the issue before, for wisdom.
- **Follow your values.** A good decision has to be in line with your values. You should have the attitude that you will always obey your values and beliefs in making a particular decision. With this settled ahead of time, you won't waiver.
- **Declare your decision.** Tell others what you have decided. Regardless of any likely consequences, you need to declare your decision. When you make values-based decisions in life, you can declare those decisions, knowing that regardless of the immediate consequences, ultimately your decisions will prove to be the best course of action.

After Bill shared this model with me, I often used it to make tough decisions. That day on the Hudson River, I had to make several tough, life-changing decisions, and Bill's model helped me.

The first came when I changed my flight from the 5:00 p.m. flight to the early afternoon flight. I was assigned seat 15A, which put me right in the middle of the plane. I didn't know it at the time, but from there I could witness what was going on when the birds struck the left engine.

When I heard the words, "Brace for impact," I did step two of the decision-making model. I withdrew. I prayed and went into my own "cocoon." I came out with a plan, and when it came time, I executed it. That plan changed when I got to the aisle. That's when I heard my mother saying, "Do the right thing, and God will be with you."

At that moment, the decisions became easier to make, such as going to the back of the plane to check on others, holding the lifeboat close to the wing so people could exit onto the wing, and making the call to jump into freezing water and swim. I made those decisions based on my values, and I declared my decisions by the actions I took. I used the model that Bill taught me, which he learned from his mentor. I had an exit strategy ready to go, like my father taught me.

Thank God my parents taught me to make decisions early in my life. When it came to the most dangerous and life-threatening time in my life, I was able to execute, assess risks, and make the correct decisions for me and, hopefully, others.

Putting It into Practice

Decision-making is the resource that will determine your destiny. The most essential step in decision-making is choosing to make a decision. Most people put off deciding things because they are afraid of making the wrong decision. As I learned from Bill, you will not make the right decision 100 percent of the time, so quit agonizing and choose. Many people I speak to focus on what they can't control and how it may not work out. What you should focus on is making a decision.

Focus on What You Can Control Today!

One of the greatest benefits I had as director of security for Tony Robbins was the opportunity to spend time with him one-on-one on international trips. During one trip to the Gold Coast in Australia, Tony and I went out to hit golf balls between sessions. It was one thing that he could do to loosen up and get his mind off things, and I was the one person on the security team who played golf and knew my way around the driving range and course.

As we were hitting balls, we started to talk about what was going on with me and why I was still working for someone else. This was a conversation we had every time I picked him up at the airport or helipad, but this time we were away from everyone and in a more casual atmosphere.

I gave him another excuse, about the money I was making, and that I really didn't know what I could do on my own that would make that kind of money. Tony told me that I needed to make a decision, and he asked what I was scared of. He then started to break down for me how I should decide to start my own business.

He told me that first I need to ask myself a different question: what should I be focusing on? I was focusing on why I couldn't do it, instead of what I could be doing to start a business. He told me that what I focus on is what I will feel. Next, he shared with me what it would mean if I had my own business. I needed to reframe the meaning of what that goal meant to me. And third, he told me that I needed to choose what I wanted to do with my life: stay where I was and be comfortable or make a decision that could change my life and my family's lives and, more importantly, others' lives.

Five years after I survived the Miracle on the Hudson, I decided that it was time to make the move, and I focused on these questions. On February 1, 2014, I made the move to start my own business. I was given the lesson and now I was ready to receive it.

Consider Others

When making decisions as a leader, it's important to remember the other people who will be affected by your choices. If Bill had concentrated his business on what he wanted instead of what his customers wanted, he might not have grown his business the way he did. If I had focused on all the bad things that could have happened after the plane crashed during the Miracle on the Hudson, I would have made different decisions that may have put me on a different path, and I may not have survived.

I gained some experience with that type of team decision-making process at a very early age in Boy Scouts, and it has served me well through my life. It doesn't mean that your team will all agree, but gauging people's opinions will help you find greater success.

This was the last dinner we ever had with my grandmother.
My mom was so happy she had her kids there with her for it.

Lesson Eleven: Build Your Best Team

April 1968

I was so excited about my first summer playing Little League baseball. I'd dreamed of this day for years. I had been working hard practicing my baseball skills and had visions of being a great shortstop and pitcher. My goal was to make the all-star team.

Our Little League chose teams by draft, and the worst team from the year before got the first pick. That spring, I was the best new player in the draft, thanks to all the drilling from my mom and dad. At our first practice, I was the only one who could catch a pitch, so I became the catcher. I wasn't happy, but one of my favorite players was Johnny Bench, so at least I took some comfort in knowing I was like him.

The season started and things went pretty well, but the coach needed me to pitch sometimes as well. When I was on the mound, he put Lee behind the plate. Lee's parents couldn't afford to get him a catcher's mitt or cleats, so I lent him my mitt for the first couple times I pitched.

After one particular game, yet another loss for our team, my mom and I stopped at the local Dairy Queen for ice cream. She knew I was frustrated, because she knew my goal was to make the all-star team later in the year, but I didn't have a good chance if our team did not perform well.

My mom took that opportunity to teach me a little about being a good teammate. She told me one way I could stand out was to help the other boys on the team learn how to play better.

"You're a great player, Dave, but baseball is a team sport," my mom said. "On a team all the players must pull their weight. You see that on teams like the Cincinnati Reds, where they all do their part to help the team succeed."

That night I had an idea. Ever since I was a little boy, I'd helped my mom collect S&H Green Stamps. Whenever she would go to the grocery store, she would get the stamps. She then gave them to me, and I put them in the stamp book and kept track of them. My reward for being her helper was using those stamps to buy athletic gear.

After our ice cream at Dairy Queen, I got out my little S&H Green Stamp book and we counted up the stamps. I had enough stamps to get a Spaulding catcher's mitt and some rubber cleats. My mom ordered them the next day. The following week I gave Lee the mitt and cleats. I don't think he ever got anything like that before, and he really didn't know what to say.

I showed him how to break the mitt in and catch with it. That was my first lesson on how to be a good teammate and build others up so all of us on the team could pull our weight.

Baseball wasn't the only sport in which I excelled. When I was a seventh grader, the ninth-grade basketball coach had already made a connection with me. That year we decided it would be best if I played on the eighth-grade team. The coaches and my dad had talked, and even though I could have made it on the ninth-grade team, I would be sitting on the bench more, and on the eighth-grade team I'd get more playing time.

I had to go through tryouts for the eighth-grade team even though I pretty much had already made the team. I was the new guy at school, and my coming in and taking a spot from someone who grew up in Winchester didn't go over too well. The same thing had happened when I played eighth-grade football in seventh grade, so I was prepared for the attitudes.

The eighth-grade coach was the guidance counselor at my junior high school, so he had some flexibility and wasn't tied to a classroom. He would spend time with me at lunch and after PE class, helping me acclimate to the new school. One day I went to his office and saw on his wall a poster of John Wooden's Pyramid of Success.

My coach told me he went to UCLA and was a John Wooden fan. These were the years of UCLA's run of ten NCAA championships. Coach would tell me how John Wooden prepared his players and his team and how the UCLA players seemed ready for any situation.

My dad saw my interest and got a book for me about John Wooden's pyramid and how he got his teams ready for the season, and I became obsessed with how he prepared his players to be the most productive players they could become. The blocks of Wooden's pyramid were important attributes a winning player and a winning person must exemplify.

The foundational bottom row included industriousness, friendship, loyalty, cooperation, and enthusiasm, which were key characteristics for anyone, not just basketball players. Stacked on top of these basics were upper-tier qualities such as self-control, initiative, skill, confidence, and poise.

Coach Wooden taught his players to adopt each quality into their character as they worked toward competitive greatness, which was the block at the top of the pyramid. Competitive greatness, in Coach Wooden's mind, was reached when you were able to "be at your best when your best is needed for your team," as he said in the book *Quotable Wooden*. To get there, he believed, you had to work through the blocks of the pyramid with consistency.

I worked on each of these attributes and mimicked each of the drills and approaches he taught, down to how to put my socks on and how to tie my shoes (and I never had a blister on my foot after I did it the John Wooden way). At our first practice, Coach sat us on the first row of the bleacher and told us to undress down to our shorts.

All of us thought it was a little weird, but he was teaching us the basics, which included how to put our socks and shoes on correctly. I realized what he was doing when we got to the socks, because I'd been reading about Wooden's philosophies, but the other teammates didn't. We did that every day for the first week, and I could tell the team was questioning why they were playing on this team.

During practice the first week, all we did was run, do the layup line, and shoot free throws. In the locker room, the other players were mad and frustrated, as they just wanted to play. I realized after a couple of practices why the coach pulled me into his office. He needed someone to be a leader on the team, to be his voice in the locker room, and to pull the team together to be the most productive they could be.

I learned a lot of things that season that served me throughout my life. Being asked to step up and share with our team what I learned from Coach Wooden and how I learned the mindset of how a champion prepares, served me then, as I grew, and especially on January 15, 2009. I learned how important it is to be on a team with players who have that mindset.

When I got my first job after graduating from James Madison University, I knew nothing about hotel/restaurant management, but I did know a little bit about being on a team. That job was a great learning ground for how to work with a team and lead different groups of people I didn't have much in common with other than work.

For the next three years, I gained experience leading and working with many teams of people who spoke other languages and had different backgrounds. I witnessed how effective teams could impact the customer experience, and therefore the bottom line, and how devastating it could be when people went their own way, apart from the team. These skill sets were invaluable to me over the next several years.

About two-and-a-half years after I started with Howard Johnson, the restaurant division was purchased by Marriott Corporation. For me, that was like being traded from the Pirates to the Yankees. Marriott had many different restaurant types and was international, much different than the corporate structure I was used to with Howard Johnson.

I was excited, as I thought I'd found my pathway to my discipline in international business. I was offered a job and put into a new store concept in which I would go to a location that was transitioning from a Howard Johnson to a Marriott or to a new store setup.

While all this was going on in my career, I proposed to my fiancée, Terri. She was a trooper during our dating relationship, as she would travel from Charlotte to see me wherever I was. The last store I was assigned to with Marriott was in Vienna, Virginia.

Then they came to me with my next move, which would have been either Baltimore or Philadelphia. This time, though, it wasn't so much a promotion—it was the same amount of money I was already making. Taking that offer would mean moving further from Charlotte. That didn't sit too well with Terri, so ultimately, I had to decide whether to leave Marriott and move back to Charlotte or go north without her.

You know by now what my decision was. As I was working out the final months of my assignment with Marriott, I was working as the first assistant manager, which meant I was second in charge of the store. That position required me to work mornings, afternoons, and nights.

Our location was right across the road from Tysons Corner Mall. On Christmas Eve 1986, we had cleaned up the restaurant after the lunch rush and were getting ready to restock, when all of a sudden, we filled up again quickly.

We were understaffed, and I was running from the front of the house to the back of the house, covering wherever I was needed. As I was moving from the back to the front of the house, I looked up and saw a contingent of well-dressed men in suits. I looked a little closer and recognized one of them.

He was Bill Marriott, the CEO of Marriott Corporation. He and his management were out visiting stores. I didn't know what to do, so I went up to him and introduced myself as the manager on duty. He looked around and asked me if everything was alright.

I said yes, then he asked me if I needed any help. I quickly evaluated how to answer. Do I say no, and have him see that everything is not alright and I'm in over my head, or say yes, and he thinks that I am not the guy for the job? I quickly decided to tell him yes, I could use some help in the back of the house, someone dropping fries.

He immediately moved toward the kitchen, but before he got there he turned to his team and told them to jump in. They began to bus tables for me while the CEO of Marriott dropped fries.

That afternoon I learned a great lesson on responsive leadership and teamwork. When all heck is breaking loose, leaders must realize they are not too big to help out and respond to the moment. I later realized when I thanked him for his help that Mr. Marriott knew his name was on the building, and ultimately the success or failure depended on pulling together and having a capable team.

Responding to the customer was as much his responsibility as it was mine or the waitresses on the floor. It was my first major lesson on how important it is to be a servant leader and how important it is to have team members who understand being productive, not just efficient.

When I left Marriott to go back to North Carolina, the first call I made was to Kinston, North Carolina. Back when I'd worked at the Howard Johnson in Wytheville, Virginia, I met Cam Cameron, a gentleman from Kinston. He was heading to Greensboro to visit one of his Bojangles stores. He asked me if I ever thought of managing a fast-food restaurant, and in case I ever wanted to, he left me his card.

I had kept that card, and I called Mr. Cameron before I left Vienna. We met in Richmond, and he told me he was going to open a new fine dining restaurant in Kinston, something one of a kind in eastern North Carolina. He asked me if I would be interested in opening it up with him, then managing it. He offered me a great package in addition to the use of one of his houses while we were opening the restaurant. I called Bill when I got back to Charlotte to bounce this off him.

I met Bill for dinner, and I told him about this opportunity. In addition to his movie theaters, Bill had some interests in a few restaurants in South Carolina. We discussed the pros and cons. I would be closer to Terri but still not in Charlotte. The money was very good, along with the perks, but I would have to work seven days a week. Cam had offered gas money for Terri to come to Kinston to visit, and he promised me a day off every couple of weeks. Bill asked me if I had a say-so over hiring my team. I told him that Cam and I didn't discuss that. This was the first time I would be working for a small company with little structure. He said that was something I should negotiate into my agreement.

Bill told me a story about when he was investing in some restaurants for the first time in the 1940s, and he shared how difficult it was. I asked him what made it more difficult than opening movie theaters. He told me that he owned most of his theaters straight up, but he was only a part owner in the restaurants.

He had a say, but he did not have the final decision on personnel. His first restaurant went belly-up, as he tried to manage it like a theater. He told me he called his mentor to get some coaching, as he was in a new field. The model he put together for his movie theaters was not working in the restaurants.

He said his mentor told him about when he started buying and managing businesses after World War I. Having one company was pretty straightforward, but when he began to expand, he realized that if he was going to be successful, he needed his management team not only to look after the bottom line but also to work as a team and be productive.

Bill's mentor taught him, "Team effectiveness is the key to having a world-class company." Bill realized he needed to have more say in personnel and to get people who understood the mission of the business into positions they excelled at. His mentor laid out for Bill a strategy on how to build an effective and efficient team.

- Focus first on the roles that have the most impact.
- Make sure each team member feels like their job matters.
- Communicate well with your team.
- Make sure each team member understands the mission.
- Always celebrate success and turn failures into learning experiences.
- Know each member of your key team.

Bill told me that he took this model and used it not only for his restaurants but also with his key teams in his theaters, and it helped him grow rapidly. Word quickly spread around that his company was a good one to work for, and the best people wanted to work with him, not for him. He told me that was a critical distinction.

I accepted the position in Kinston. I saw it as a great opportunity, and I used Bill's strategy to work to build a team that would be world-class for eastern North Carolina. After about six weeks, I started to realize that what happened to Bill in his first restaurant ventures was happening to me. Cam brought his sister in to oversee personnel, and now I had only small input on who would be on the team.

I knew we needed to recruit from outside the area if we were going to have the quality restaurant Cam wanted, but his sister wasn't seeing eye to eye with me. If I hadn't learned that lesson from Bill's mentor via Bill, I might not have been able to make the call to leave Kinston and begin my career in sales. Teamwork matters. I knew that without the right team in place, I wouldn't be able to succeed, and since my hands were tied, it was time for a change.

Teamwork doesn't just happen in sports or in your job. Working as a team is a mentality that can help you succeed in relationships and in life. That's a lesson I learned one week after my experience on the Hudson. One of the benefits I received after the Miracle on the Hudson was the opportunity to meet and talk with airline captains and first officers.

The week after the plane crash I was traveling again, this time to Orlando. I was upgraded to first class on my way back to Charlotte, and as I was waiting to board, the captain of the upcoming flight was also waiting. I make it a habit of thanking the captain, first officer, and crew for what they do to get me to where I am going. That day I thanked the captain as we waited, and he acknowledged me and asked if I was one of those passengers on the plane that day. I told him yes, and we struck up a conversation.

As we were discussing the events from that day, he brought up something I hadn't thought about. He asked me what was going on inside the cabin as the plane started its final descent into the Hudson River. I told him it was eerily quiet. He asked me if I had seen the movie Flight with Denzel Washington, and I told him yes, I had. He then made a distinction that confirmed not only some of my thoughts about teamwork but also the importance of being a part of a team that was effective.

He said that in the movie, the flight was going from Orlando to Atlanta, and when the plane started to go down, there was chaos with the passengers inside the cabin. "If I'd had to do what the captain of US Airways Flight 1549 did that day, but on a flight out of Orlando, there would have been a completely different outcome," he said.

"Why is that?" I asked.

"Look around," he said. I did. The people getting ready to board the plane that day were families, older adults, people going on vacation. There were only a few people like me—business travelers.

"This is a typical flight out of Orlando, but your passenger makeup out of LaGuardia is usually different. During the week, it's mostly business travelers," he said. "How many families or people on vacation were with you on that flight that crashed?"

"I don't know, but I do remember an elderly lady and a family."

"The passenger makeup of the plane has everything to do with the outcome," he said. "Businesspeople are taught to handle themselves and solve problems quickly. Vacationers and families don't focus on those things."

He told me his thoughts about what happened on January 15, 2009: that there were two miracles. One was with the captain and first officer making the decision to land on the river, and the second was with the passengers managing the exit process. This was not only a new way to think about what happened and how miracles occur, but it was also a great illustration of teamwork. By having a team that is focused on the mission and on being effective and efficient, you can accomplish just about anything, even a miracle.

Putting It into Practice

Finding success in life isn't a one-person accomplishment. Your success depends on the support of your personal team and the goals you accomplish together. Whether it's your life partner, your work colleagues, or a volunteer opportunity, finding the right team is important for success.

When you choose your team, you'll want to look for team members who will focus on the mission of the organization, want to be a part of something bigger than themselves, are open to giving and receiving feedback, and have the skills and capability to execute.

Ask the Right Questions

A couple of years ago I was asked, "What did you learn being a leader of a team for Tony Robbins that helped you during the Miracle on the Hudson?" It was an excellent question.

Every time I added a new person to our security team, I asked three questions:

- Can this person do the job?
- Will they do their responsibilities well for the long term?
- Do they culturally fit into the team?

I'm forever grateful to Tony for having the confidence in me to lead a group of leaders. People on that team were owners of businesses or leaders in their companies who, like me, were volunteering their time to work with Tony. They were willing to check their egos at the door and focus on the mission at hand every day. We worked at a demanding pace, but each member of the team raised their standards every day and met our goals.

They taught me many things that helped me help other people on that fateful day of January 15, 2009. When the passengers had to manage the entire situation on the right side of the plane, leaders among us stepped up. Some checked their egos at the door so that others could execute, and all focused on the single mission of the day: survival. Together, we achieved an outcome that was truly a miracle.

Raise Your Standards

As director of security for Tony Robbins, my mission was not only to support and protect Tony so he could serve at his highest level but also to lead a team of people who were committed to being outstanding at every event. I wanted people on the team who would raise our standards each time. By raising our standards, the team and individuals would become better and stronger together.

Raising our standards simply meant turning things the team should do into must do. Turning your shoulds into musts can change your outlook, improving how your team produces and making your personal life better.

One of my responsibilities at every event was to make sure Tony could spend time with this elite group of leaders on our security team. Each member of the team was a leader in his company or a business owner. Learning to lead these leaders was one of my greatest lessons while serving Tony.

Lesson Twelve: Poise under Pressure

October 1971

During our weekly Scout meetings, Scoutmaster Walker would always have an adventure set up for us. Our lodge was in the woods, so a lot of the adventures had us going out to find or make something or figuring out how to get back to the lodge without a flashlight. As I advanced through the different badge levels, the adventures increased in difficulty. We not only had to use our physical strengths, but we also had to use and manage our minds.

On this particular night in October, Scoutmaster Walker sent us out after dark into the woods to find some Indian artifacts he had put out. We were to use them to get back to the lodge without a flashlight. I was a First-Class Scout, and the woods and the Scout hut were right behind my house, so I had a lot of experience in this terrain and knew it well.

That night was cold, the paths were covered with fallen leaves, and it was dark. Our team was anxious, but we knew we had to keep our minds in the game to get back to the hut by the time our parents came to pick us up. We didn't have a compass, so we put things on the trees to mark our way, but those were hard to see in the dark. All of us started to worry a little, but we ultimately got back with the Indian artifacts.

To parents in this day and age, that might seem like a pretty tough exercise for a group of kids, but if you know how, where, and when Mr. Walker grew up, his type of leadership made sense. Mr. Walker grew up in the early decades of the twentieth century in rural southern Ohio.

He was enamored with Scouting and the military. He earned his Eagle Scout in a community where no one really knew what it meant or what you had to do to earn it. At that time there was little or no technology, so he had to be creative and use his hands and his wit to accomplish all the goals to get to Eagle. He wanted us to have those same experiences because he knew how it had served him, setting him up for success as an adult.

As Scoutmaster Walker and I were putting together the application for me to attend the Order of the Arrow recognition, I asked him about that adventure. He told me something that not only served me during the Order of the Arrow weekend but many times throughout my life since, especially on January 15, 2009.

He told me that part of being an Eagle Scout was having the ability to manage your emotions and be composed with whatever life tosses your way. Going out in the cold, dark woods with very little information and having to use my own skills to survive became a metaphor for me. It taught me that when things got tough, if I stayed composed, I could ultimately get the outcome I desired.

During my ninth-grade basketball season, things were going well. I was a starter, and my stats were in the double digits, but I had one issue I had to battle. I fouled a lot. Our coach, Les Cummings, kept telling me if I wanted to stay on the court, I needed to calm down and back off a little, but that was hard for me. I played every sport with intensity, like it was game seven and I was Pete Rose. All out, with no tomorrow.

About midway through the season, I snapped at an official and received a technical foul. I took the bench and got a talking-to from Coach Cummings. The next game was at Warren County, and once again I got a foul, I didn't think I deserved. I snapped at the official and got a technical.

Again, I was pulled to the bench and got a lecture from the coach.

When we got back to school the next day, Coach Rogers, the junior varsity coach at James Wood High School, called me to his classroom. He had a TV, so I thought we were going to watch videos from the game, and he was going to give me some pointers, as I would be at the high school next year and possibly playing for him. I sat down, and he told me to watch.

The video was of Bjorn Borg playing John McEnroe in tennis. McEnroe was blowing up while Borg was composed and poised—a stark contrast. I watched closely and listened to the commentators' praise Borg and say how McEnroe needed to grow up.

After the video was done, Coach Rogers told me I needed to have composure off and on the court. People were watching me at all times as a leader on the team, and people would watch me more for how I handled myself than for my skills. He knew he would probably be my coach the next year, which was why he spent a lot of time training me.

This was a personal talk, not a coach talk. I got the message. I didn't have any incidents the rest of the year, and I learned another lesson about how important it is to have poise and maintain composure when bad things happen.

The next year, Coach Rogers took a head coaching job at his alma mater in Martinsburg, West Virginia, which meant he wouldn't be my coach in high school. I was disappointed but still gave my all to the team. I was excelling on the junior varsity team, but my problem with fouling resurfaced. During a game at Garfield, I snapped at the official, and he gave me a technical. I got pulled out of the game and sat for the rest of the quarter.

I looked up, and my dad and my mom were shaking their heads. My mom knew I went into an intense mode on game day, and now it was showing up on the court. When I got home that evening my mom told me I needed to get it together, that my attitude was going to hold me back if I didn't.

The next day at school the varsity head coach, Donnie Hambleton, called me to his classroom between classes. He was a government teacher, and I excelled in history, civics, and government, so I thought it might be about something in those areas.

He closed the door behind me and sat me down and told me he saw how I reacted on the court—and if I was going to play for him and wanted an opportunity to play in college, I needed to learn to manage my temper. He gave me a book and told me to read it and write a book report on it.

The book was Clyde: The Walt Frazier Story. Clyde Frazier played for the New York Knicks and was a fantastic guard. He never lost his cool, even when people antagonized him or knocked him around. Coach Hambleton was a big New York Knicks fan and loved Clyde Frazier. I read the book and did the report for Coach Hambleton, and I learned a lesson along the way. Especially in sports, people will do just about anything to get under your skin. If you are going to be a standout player, you need to learn to play with poise, have composure, and, most importantly, smile through challenging times. It was another lesson that would serve me on January 15, 2009.

In 1996, I took a position with BMS. That company focused on the small to medium market for HR and payroll services. I was brought on by a former employer of mine who was now working there. The position was great for me, as I was back in smaller businesses compared to the national account position I had at my last job at ADP, where I worked with the largest companies in the Carolinas. I started quickly and made a few sales. It felt good to be back in the game and having success.

After a great week of prospecting and sales, I was ready to have a relaxing weekend with my family. Friday evening when I got home, there was a certified letter addressed to me. It was a letter from an attorney at ADP reminding me of the noncompete clause in my sales agreement with ADP, informing me I needed to cease and desist from selling at BMS. I took the letter into the office in Charlotte on Monday and showed it to my boss. He told me ADP always does that when someone leaves, and not to worry about it. I let it go and didn't respond.

A couple of weeks later, I received another certified letter with the same message, stating if I didn't cease and desist, ADP would sue me. I had never seen a letter like that before. I took that letter into work and showed it to Gordon, my senior sales executive, and Mike, the owner of BMS. Both told me I shouldn't worry, but I needed to respond and let them know why I wasn't in breach of the agreement. They both recommended I get an attorney to make it look official.

Terri knew an attorney whom she had used when she had a car wreck, so I called him. He agreed to write a letter for me, charging $1,000 to handle it. It was at that moment I learned how expensive attorneys could be. I agreed, and he wrote and sent the letter. I felt better, but it was always on my mind. I wasn't as effective in my work because of the nagging worry.

A few weeks later, I received another certified letter threatening me with breach of contract, stating if I didn't cease working with BMS I would be sued. After I received that third letter, my worry turned to anger, and I called Bill to get some counsel.

I met Bill at his office and took all the ADP letters and the letter the attorney sent on my behalf. He told me that it was a scare tactic, but I had to take it seriously, as ADP had infinite resources.

"If you don't do what you need to do to handle this situation, they could bleed you dry," Bill said. That wasn't too uplifting, but then Bill shared something that happened to him, which help put things in perspective for me.

"During the war years in the early '40s, my theaters were all making money," Bill said. "I had the assets to keep my expansion plans going, so I opened more theaters in the counties around Charlotte and in South Carolina. In 1943 I took a risk on something other than a movie theater—

opening my first restaurants in South Carolina. They started to pick up steam, so I had plans to open more."

Just as Bill was really gaining traction with his new theaters and restaurants, he got a letter from an attorney. The letter said his restaurant concept was too similar to a franchise that was also expanding throughout the East Coast, and it said he needed to cease and desist and close his restaurants or change the concept.

Bill called his mentor and asked for his advice. His mentor told him that as a successful business owner, he was always going to have someone coming after him. No one kicks a dead dog, and he needed to think about the long-term win and stay composed. Don't let anyone see him rattled. He couldn't just ignore it. His mentor told Bill to get his ducks in a row and respond, but not to dwell on it if he was in the right. Bill told me that it was a great lesson for him while he was growing his business. Learning to think about the long term while maintaining his composure helped him stay calm.

Bill also told me something he'd read about Winston Churchill.

"The great question before him initially was how to keep his naval forces afloat during the turbulence of the early days of the war," Bill said. "In less than a year, Churchill's great concern would turn to holding the Parliament and country on an even keel as Nazi assaults pounded them.

To do that, he needed to keep the nation calm, a goal he would accomplish with his speeches and with his own demeanor of relentless optimism and composure. Churchill's personality and character would be crucial elements to keeping the citizens of Britain calm. He demonstrated personally how to 'keep calm and carry on.' The challenges he faced in forming a new government revealed the gigantic size of the task."

Bill asked me if I was in the right in this instance. I told him yes. I was working out of an office in Columbia, South Carolina, over sixty miles away from the offices in Charlotte. Plus, I was working in the small and medium market, which was different than the large national accounts I had served with ADP, so I would not be directly competing with ADP. Bill told me that should be sufficient and not to respond anymore to ADP. "Keep the long game in mind and stay calm," he said.

The next week I went back to work at BMS. I drove 180 miles a day for a year from Charlotte to Columbia and back, heads-down on building a business. I never again responded to ADP and never received another letter.

That year I became salesperson of the year at BMS, all by keeping the long game in mind and maintaining my composure. That mindset set me on a path for more significant and challenging opportunities in the future.

Learning this lesson served me well as my US Airways flight started to cross over the George Washington Bridge, heading nose first into the ice-cold Hudson River.

One of the questions I am asked most often about my experience on Flight 1549 is, "How does someone really manage their mind through a crisis?" I share something I first learned in 1994 at a Tony Robbins event, Date with Destiny. I employed it on January 15, 2009, during and after the plane crash.

Before that event I was spending time with Tony at his Namale Resort in Fiji. We were on the way to jump off a bridge into a natural salt river in the middle of the night. The distance between the bridge and the salt river was pretty significant. However, once a person gets the courage to jump, they land in the warm saltwater and float into the darkness under the stars, and they eventually end up in a beautiful saltwater lagoon.

On the drive up to the bridge, anticipating the jump we were about to experience, Tony and I were talking about how to stay composed when your mind is going wild. Tony told me, "You've got to put yourself in a state of resourcefulness and gratitude."

Once we reached the bridge and it was my time to jump, I couldn't see anything below me. I realized that I had to change what I focused on and stay composed. I started to put myself in a resourceful state. I had a magic moment coming up, and I had gratitude for everything I had in my life, especially my family.

I regained my composure and jumped off that bridge, beneath a starlit black sky into the salt river about fifty feet below. Once I came up and started to float down the river, I realized that most of the time in life, we put fear into our heads that is not really there. This experience is a reference I consistently use when things start to go sideways.

As the plane started to approach the George Washington Bridge, I could see that what was happening was one of those moments. In the next ninety seconds, I could be dead or severely injured or burned. As the movie of my life passed through my mind with clarity, I quickly saw that moment on the bridge in Fiji. When I looked up for the last time before impact, I wasn't scared, and I immediately knew that what Tony and Bill told me was correct. I went into a mindset of gratitude and became composed.

I thought about the long-term win I would have, either with my family or in heaven. Fortunately for me, I survived the impact of the plane hitting the water. I remained composed and focused during the evacuation of the aircraft, on the ferry, at the Weehawken terminal, and at Palisades Medical Center where finally, through maintaining my composure with gratitude, I survived a plane crash. That moment was not lost on me, and now I have a new chance at life and can fulfill the commitment I made to Bill in 1997.

Putting It into Practice

Once you learn how to think about the long-term win and stay composed, you can help others step up. Everybody throughout their lives will face what I call a "personal plane crash" moment—your PITTChE. It could be a heart attack, stroke, car accident, cancer, loss of a job, death of a family member, or even a plane crash. If you lose your head, you lessen your chances of surviving that moment. Successful leaders have learned to keep their heads when everyone around them is losing theirs.

Find Your State of Gratitude

It all starts with putting yourself in a state of gratitude, being thankful for something or someone bigger than you are and thinking of all the resources you have available. As I learned from Tony, it's not about the resources you don't have; it's about the resourcefulness you do have. Once you put yourself in a resourceful state, gratitude kicks in, you know all will turn out well, and you have a chance for that long-term victory!

Communicate with Yourself in Times of Crisis

So many people think that when you talk to yourself, it's a sign you're losing your mind, but I believe it's exactly the opposite. I have had the opportunity to share the stage and speak with experts in different fields, including law enforcement professionals and military experts such as Army Rangers and Navy SEALs.

I've asked them, when things are happening so quickly, especially in life and death situations, how does someone execute? One thing I learned from my own experience is communicating with yourself under pressure is a critical leadership component. Almost 100 percent of those professionals agreed.

We all agreed that in the moment, whether you are going down in a plane crash, facing off with a felon, or going to get a terrorist, starting with a prayer of gratitude, and having the ability to talk yourself through the situation is where it begins.

Without the ability to maintain composure, think clearly, assess the potential risks while gathering information, and make the call, your odds of succeeding are massively reduced, which, of course, can lead to the worst possible outcome. To raise your odds of success and/or survival, stay composed by saying a prayer of gratitude. Remember to also thank your team and loved ones for the opportunity to serve before you begin.

My varsity basketball coach, Donnie Hambleton, preached to me about keeping my composure at all times. As with many people, sometimes it's "Do as I say, not as I do!"

Lesson Thirteen: The Real Lesson

August 7, 2021

I survived the plane crash on the Hudson, but I did not come out of it unscathed. In the months and years following that fateful day, I often thought of one of the things Bill often said to me, "There will be lessons to learn in life, but patience is the key. People who have patience will not be desperate."

I knew I had to have patience with myself after that day on the Hudson, patience with my new anxiety around traveling, patience with my hesitancy to leave home and be away from my wife and children. That patience also helped me find a way to triumph over my turmoil of emotions.

I remembered something from one of my first Jim Rohn seminars in Dallas, Texas, in 1988. He said, "Stop wearing your raincoat in the shower." You cannot let your fears take over your life and live in your head, as it will constantly put you in a state of uncertainty. The pathway to turning your turmoil into triumph is to shed your raincoat of uncertainty and fear, face your demon head-on, and move on to certainty. All of this takes patience and faith.

The week following the Miracle on the Hudson, my regional manager asked me to travel. As I prepared to get on another plane, I was asked by my co-workers, friends, and even strangers, “Why would you do that?” In fact, I asked myself that same question. Why? Because I knew I needed to do it. I couldn’t stand in the shower in my raincoat forever—I had to get on with my life.

Of course, that first flight was challenging, but that was also the day I initially faced and overcame any potential fear and uncertainty I had. Taking that leap of faith allowed me to meet many outstanding people and to find and live the purpose of my life.

On January 15, 2009, one hundred fifty-five people who didn’t know each other or care about each other pulled together to do something that had never been done before. That’s one of the key things that came out of that day: when you have a mission and have commonality of that mission, you can achieve anything.

That lesson was brought home to me in another way in the spring of 2021.

I have always been a good swimmer. My mother got me in swimming lessons as a child in 1966, and earlier in this book I wrote how she pushed me to get my junior lifeguard certification. My mother believed swimming is a skill every child should have because it is not only a useful exercise, but it is also a skill that could save your life. She turned out to be right about that. On January 15, 2009, I had to swim to get off a sinking airplane that had crashed into the Hudson River.

As I swam out of the Hudson to save my life, I never thought I would go into that cold water again—until April 2021, when I took a call from my friend Suzanne. She was going to do the Navy SEAL Hudson River Swim and Run and asked me if I would be interested in going back.

"It might give you some sense of redemption," Suzanne said.

"Sure. Put me in touch with the person in charge," I said. A few days later I got a call from Scuba, who was going to help train me. Scuba told me to meet him at MSA Swimming in Marvin, North Carolina, at 5:00 a.m. It turns out that was my first test, to see if I'd show up that early in the morning.

I showed up at 5:00 a.m. in my swim trunks, ready to go. Scuba cleared his swim lane and asked me to swim to the other end. I made it to the end, but I was extremely winded, and my head was beet red. We had three months to train.

"I'm not going to take you out of this swim, you will take yourself out of it, but you have a lot of work to do!" Scuba said. "The Hudson is no joke!"

The next day, I was back at the pool at 7:00 a.m., where Scuba introduced me to Coach Patty. Coach Patty is a former collegiate champion swimmer and headmasters swim coach at MSA Swimming. Scuba asked her to watch me swim one length of the pool, twenty-five meters. This time I couldn't get to the other end of the pool. Patty shook her head and reluctantly took me on as her new project.

Coach Patty told me to show up at 5:00 a.m. so I could relearn how to swim. For the next fifteen weeks, she watched and coached with patience, breaking my swimming form down stroke by stroke and step by step.

She made a list of everything I needed, and I quickly found out that swim equipment is not inexpensive. I hadn't budgeted for it, but I bought everything she asked me to get. I learned years ago from both Bill and Tony, never question someone who is world-class or a coach who has major accomplishments, as they have walked their talk.

There were times when I am sure she looked at me and thought, "What did I get myself into?" but I knew she had a bigger mission as well, as she has a soft part in her heart for the military. The SEAL Swim is a fundraiser for GIGO fund, which raises money for veterans in need. Coach Patty threw her heart into support for those women and men who put themselves on the line every moment of every day for our own freedoms. Coach Patty was all in, and so was I.

Coach Patty brought in other coaches at MSA Swimming to support me. Coach Cassie was with me on day four and probably thought she would have to jump in to save me. Coach Patty constructed a swim stick so I could use it to focus on swimming straight. The Stick was like my American Express card—I didn't leave home without it. It became my certainty in the water.

My first big test was on June 1, when Patty and Cassie took me with their group to Lake Wylie. We were going to swim eight hundred meters in open water. I had swum in lakes before, but never for distance, just for fun. She told me to bring my fins, neoprene shorts, buoy, and The Stick. Coach

Patty stayed with me the entire time, and we completed eight hundred meters.

After that, we were at Lake Wylie at 7:40 a.m. every Wednesday to train for swimming in open water. The next test was one mile. I passed that test. The next week, we went all the way to Survivor Island, one mile out and one mile back. I passed that test. The week after that was the first time, I was going to do a three-mile swim, the same length as the SEAL Swim. I passed that test. I was extremely tired, but it gave me the confidence I could go the distance.

The next week, I skipped training with Coach Patty to swim with Suzanne, who was going to be my wingman on the Hudson. Suzanne was recovering from knee surgery and was getting back into the water to train. She showed me how to get my fins on in deep water, and we swam in the pool. When we finished, we went out for breakfast, and I knew we had a bond. She was going to be there for me, and I was going to be there for her. We were all in together.

A few weeks later, Coach Patty and I did our final dress rehearsal at Lake Wylie where we practiced sighting, refueling, pacing, and flipping from freestyle to backstroke. I finished, feeling strong. She knew I could swim the distance, and her confidence buoyed me. The lake was not the Hudson River, but she had helped me build the endurance and certainty that I needed to make the 3.1 mile swim in the Hudson.

The entire time I was doing the physical and mental training for the SEAL Swim, my team was focused on helping get the message out about the GIGO Fund. At one point I flew to New Jersey with two other team members, Heidi and Ivan, to produce a video to promote the reason I was doing this training and the importance of the GIGO Fund. Our focus was clear. This wasn't about me and my journey; it was about the veterans who needed support.

August 6 was a big day. Suzanne was waiting for us in New Jersey, and my family and Coach Patty joined her. Before I went back to swim in the Hudson River, my family and I went to Palisades Medical Center, where I went after I was rescued from the Hudson, to reunite with the team that saved my life.

The day of the swim I was up early. I did a workout, packed my bag, then waited for the bus. We arrived at Liberty State Park in a police escort. It reminded me of the trip I took on January 15, 2009, and the police escort from Palisades Medical Center to LaGuardia. That was the last time I had a police escort, and the feelings started to build as they had the day after the US Airways Flight 1549 crash-landed in the Hudson River.

Suzanne and I jumped into the registration line, where we got our official SEAL Swim bag. I was assigned number 154. I immediately thought this was a great sign: I was on US Airways Flight 1549, in seat 15A, on January 15, 2009. The number fifteen was with me again this day!

During the opening ceremonies I was filled with pride and emotion as they played the national anthem, said a prayer, and recited the Pledge of Allegiance. About an hour later, we were ready to go. It was truly go time!

We initially thought we were walking into the Hudson River, which would give Suzanne and me the chance to acclimate to the cold water and allow me to get warmed up and into my rhythm. That game plan went out the window immediately when we were told we would be jumping thirteen feet off the ledge of a bridge into the Hudson.

I had practiced jumping into the water, so I had my game plan for that, but Suzanne hadn't. She jumped in first, then I jumped in and did my tuck and roll. All was good until I could not find Suzanne—she was already floating out into the river. There was no time to warm up, no time for finding a rhythm, as I had to catch up to Suzanne.

The first lesson I took away from the swim was that you can have all the strategy and best planning, but sometimes strategy goes out the window and you must adapt and get resourceful very quickly. Just like that day the plane crashed; my training came to help when the plan went out the window.

Scuba told us the first leg was the toughest, as the current was against us. He pointed out our sightings before we jumped in, but after we were in the water and the tide was high, it took a few minutes to find Suzanne and the sightings Scuba pointed out.

I started out with the game plan Coach Patty, and I put together before the swim to catch up with Suzanne: swim twenty strokes freestyle with my swim stick, flip over, attach The Stick to my buoy and backstroke twenty strokes, flip over, get my sightings by kicking, and repeat. After my first twenty freestyle strokes, I turned over on my back and realized the carabiner Coach Patty had put on my stick was gone. Luckily, she had put on a backup carabiner, so I clipped it on and backstroked to find Suzanne.

A New Jersey State trooper found my carabiner and swam up to get close enough to throw it at me. I tried to swim to it, but the current was so strong it was being carried in the opposite direction. I was trying to catch up with Suzanne the entire first leg, but I never did. About five hundred meters out from the barge, a trooper on a jet ski told me to hold on and took me up to meet Suzanne, who was about two hundred meters away. He dropped me off in the water and I began swimming to the barge. Suzanne was making her way also, but we never connected in the water.

I got to the barge about two minutes before she did. We had to climb up the ladder after we got our fins off. That was a struggle, but I got to the top first and watched Suzanne climb up, knowing her knee situation, and she had to go up slowly. The crew and I helped her on the barge and then we debriefed and put another strategy in place.

We did fifty push-ups, and I refueled with the gels I had put in my suit. We met a new friend, Jessica, who was swimming alone, and we decided to climb down the ladder on the side of the barge so we could make sure we stayed together, instead of jumping another fifteen feet off the front. We had an additional twenty-five to fifty meters to swim to get to the front of the barge, but at least we were together going forward.

The second leg was to swim from the Statute of Liberty to Ellis Island. The current was strong and came at us at an angle, so if we caught it right, it took us forward. Suzanne and I went straight to Ellis Island, going freestyle to backstroke, never stopping, making it there in good shape. We again debriefed, refueled, and did push-ups.

Then we found Jessica. She had thrown up two times and was shivering. She collapsed to the floor, and Suzanne and I went to get a medic to help. We knew we had to get going to catch up to the SEALs, so we left Jessica with the medic, climbed down the ladder on the side, and started off toward Battery Park in New York City.

Scuba again helped us with our sightings. He told us to go toward the church with the green roof, where the current would help us get to the final stop. Suzanne and I started out, and the current was strong. She and I stayed together and talked throughout the leg. As we progressed to Battery Park, the current started to get stronger, and we got separated. Then a jet ski came up to Suzanne, and the driver asked her to jump on.

A few seconds later, a New York state trooper came up to me on his boat and told me, "The river will be back open for commercial traffic in about thirty minutes, and we have to clear the channel."

A boat came up to me, and the people on board asked me to hold on so they could take me to Suzanne. After about one hundred meters we caught up with Suzanne's jet ski, and we both dropped back into the water with about 350 meters to go. We swam close together for that last leg. After about one hundred meters I yelled out to Suzanne, and she said, "I'm here."

"Thank you, and I love you, Suzanne," I yelled to her.

She yelled back, "I love you too," as we came in together to Battery Park in New York City.

Suzanne asked me to climb up first. I got up and waited to help her over the ladder. I looked over and saw my family, Coach Patty, Kelli (my co-worker and executive assistant), and her boyfriend Tony, cheering for me. I was filled with so much gratitude for everyone who had gotten me to this point. I came out of the Hudson River again—but this time I was triumphant.

The event wasn't over. We had to get to the finish line at the 9/11 memorial.

Suzanne and I rode a cart to the memorial, as we could not run with the SEALs. We met them there and participated in the final ceremony. Both of us received our United States flags and carried the flags to where the World Trade Center towers went down, praying as we remembered those who lost their lives on September 11, 2001.

In the crowd that gathered at the closing ceremony, Scuba came to find me. He grabbed me and hugged me and told me how proud he was of me. That was the first time I started to get emotional. He then reached down into his bag and put a SEAL Challenge Coin in my hand and told me again how proud of me he was. He asked me to keep swimming with him and his team at MSA.

I'm filled with emotions even now as I think about what our entire team accomplished. It started as something to do to help those vets who have fallen on hard times, but it quickly turned into a mission. I had resigned myself to turmoil being part of my life from that fateful day on, but this was a way to take the turmoil and turn it into a final triumph. This time I left the river on my terms.

Initially, I thought getting out of the river was the point at which I had my redemption—redemption from the feelings that had followed me since the crash on January 15, redemption from that first day at MSA Swimming and training, redemption from feelings of self-doubt. Whatever turmoil I ever had was now a triumph.

But that was not the moment.

Earlier I wrote that many people assume the plane crash was the moment I found the purpose of my life, but it wasn't. The moment was when the elderly lady came up to me at my church and showed me how I could make a difference.

The moment I got my redemption and triumph was not when I got out of the Hudson River at Battery Park, as many people would think.

The moment was about 250 meters out from Battery Park when I told Suzanne I loved her, and she told me she loved me. That was the moment when I realized that the real redemption and pathway from turmoil to triumph involves forgiveness and giving and receiving love. That was the moment that whatever turmoil I had during and after the Miracle on the Hudson was gone.

I realized that there were so many people throughout my life who gave me forgiveness and love that helped me get to this point. My parents loved me to give me the discipline and lessons to help me become a man and a father. Bill loved me to give me fourteen years of his life to teach me the lessons that those who loved him taught him. That is why he made me promise him that I would not let what he taught me die with me.

Tony honored and loved me, asking me to have his back and teaching me distinctions to have a life of fulfillment and service. Don, my current mentor, honored me and loved me to give me the advice and lessons on how to become the servant leader I have become.

Suzanne loved me to be my swim buddy and wingman, the person who will not ever leave in my defining moments, the toughest moments in life. Another wingman in my life, Rania, is a person on my team who shows her love by being there whenever I need someone to talk to and share the challenges life presents.

I found that the pathway from turmoil to triumph begins with loving yourself first and holding yourself to a high standard. Accept that life will throw you curve balls, but if you give love and accept love from others, you will always triumph.

My mission is now to show others how they, too, can turn whatever turmoil they have had into a triumph. As Bill and Tony taught me, always find a mentor who has walked their talk, and they will lead you to victory.

All the moments in your life do matter. I am now redeemed.

Suzanne and I in the Hudson River with about 400 meters to go.

Conclusion: Revealing Your PITTChE

I believe everyone has a distinct advantage. Bill saw something distinct in me, and he was patient enough to help me find it. Hopefully, through this book and Bill's lessons you have come to learn more about your own distinct advantage. Once you understand that, it will reveal your PITTChE, the Point In Time That Changes Everything.

When I was growing up, I had a little book in which my mom collected my important keepsakes—awards, mentions in the paper, report cards, the stuff of growing up. Every year, I wrote in that book what I wanted to be when I grew up. All the way back in second grade I wrote that I wanted to be a baseball player. I loved baseball. It was my life.

Over the years, my idea of what I wanted to be when I grew up changed. The older we get, as the moments start to accumulate, our goals and ambitions change, but one thing that hasn't changed for me is my love of the game.

I may not have become a Major League Baseball player, but it's still part of my life. If you talk with my friends, they'll tell you I often tell stories and make points using sports analogies. So, as I have had the opportunity to travel the world speaking, working with people who are looking for their moment, their time, I started thinking about those times in baseball terms.

If you know anything about baseball, you know it all starts with the pitcher making a pitch. Imagine you're a baseball player, standing at the plate, waiting for the pitcher to make that pitch. The future of the game is in your hands. Anything can happen, just like anything can happen in life.

The first pitch comes along. Outside. Ball one. You didn't want that one anyway. Often the top players take the first pitch and find success, even with an outside ball, but not you, not on this one. Maybe it's a job you weren't interested in, maybe someone who wanted to date you, but you didn't share the same feelings. Pass.

Second pitch. Caught a corner. Strike one. You weren't ready, but in life, bad things happen. You got a strike. It happens even to the best hitters, but they don't walk away.

It's only one strike. They know there's more opportunity out there. You rub a little dirt on your hands and get ready for the next one.

Third pitch. Another ball. You were ready for this one but didn't swing. Sometimes knowing when to pass on something is as important as knowing when to swing.

Fourth pitch, and this one look good. You are ready and you take a big swing—and whiff. Strike two. The longer you live, the more you learn that to be successful, you must take chances. Sometimes you fail, sometimes you succeed, but all the time you can learn from your experiences. The pitch looked good, but it went past you. Accept, adjust, and advance in preparation for the next chance.

The fifth pitch comes, and this one looks good too. You swing and connect. The ball sails into the sky. Going, going, going, gone - foul. You have learned in life to accept, adjust, and advance. Even when things look like they're going well, sometimes you hit roadblocks. As long as you are in the batter's box, as long as you are conscious, you have confidence that another pitch is coming your way, another shot at success.

The count's at two and two—two balls, two strikes. You're still in the game. Here's the windup, and another pitch.

This time, you are ready. You swing, and the ball explodes off the bat. It's going, going, going, gone. Home run. You brought in the winning run! The crowd goes nuts, your team is jumping up and down, and they're waiting for you at the plate to slap you with high fives.

Before that last pitch, you were just one of the team. Then the pitch you really wanted came and was yours to hit. It was your moment, your Point In Time That Changed Everything for you. It was your PITTChE, and you took it.

After my experiences on the Hudson River, both surviving a plane crash and swimming with the Navy SEALs, I started to think about what really happened that day. I realized there are strategies that great players and great leaders must take to take advantage of that Point In Time That Changed Everything!

Most people think my PITTChE was when I survived the plane crash. but it was actually a little later than that. It wasn't when Clint Eastwood made the movie Sully. It wasn't when I was on the plane praying to God as we silently flew toward the river. My PITTChE happened a few days after the crash on January 15, 2009. I realized that all the moments in life matter and make up who you are, so you are ready to act in that defining moment, that Point

In Time That Changes Everything, and all of us have those moments.

Baseball is a game, but life isn't. Things will happen that you can't control, such as COVID-19, social unrest, elections, plane crashes. It's how you respond in those moments that define you. Everything happens for a reason and a purpose, and it serves you. You connected with that ball, not because you happened to be in the right place at the right time, but because everything in your life led you to that moment and prepared you to take that pitch and knock it out of the park. Maybe your PITTChE hasn't happened yet. Maybe you need to make it happen.

The important thing to remember is that if you don't take a swing, you'll never hit the ball out of the park. I knew at that moment a few days after the plane crash what my PITTChE was: to share my story, to use it to help others achieve their greatest goals, to help others be the best people and best leaders they can be. My mission is simple: help those who may be going through their own turmoil throughout their lives to find a pathway to victory and triumph.

Through sharing my story and life experiences, I hope you see how, in the most defining moments of our lives, the basic tenets of personal leadership, resourcefulness, and decision-making come to the forefront through focused execution, empowered by resourcefulness and transformed by gratitude. It is in those moments the leader inside you is revealed, and you see what you are called to be.

You never know when your PITTChE is coming. I sure didn't know what was coming as I boarded the plane that day—that within thirty minutes I'd go from settling in for my flight to swimming for my life in thirty-six-degree water. Bill and Tony had helped me find my own distinct advantage over the years, but it was in those moments on the plane and the time in those few days after when I found my PITTChE.

Epilogue

Why Me?

Every weekday during the COVID-19 pandemic, when we were all sheltering in place and most people were living pretty isolated lives, I made it a practice to call five people a day to check in with them. It's not only helped me keep everything in perspective for myself, but it gave me the opportunity to reengage with people I may not have spoken to otherwise.

I connected with people from all points in my life, including some I hadn't talked to in twenty years. Recently I touched base with one of my friends from the days when I was serving on the Tony Robbins security team, and she asked me a question that I had never been asked. She had been following me on social media and had been reading my posts and articles, so she had some background to draw from.

Her question to me was, "Why do you think Bill asked you to be his mentee in 1983 and trusted you to pass on his lessons?"

I carefully thought through how to answer that. At first, I got emotional when I thought about that question, as I'm sure there were many other women and men, he could have spent an excessive amount of time and patience with, time away from his family, but he chose me. What was it about me that caused Bill to ask me to drive his blue Corvette that December day?

After much thought, I finally figured out how to answer her question. I told her a story Bill told me when I was still managing hotels and restaurants.

After Bill opened his first movie theater in 1929, he had an itchto open more. His mentor told him to get the first one solid before he considered opening any more. A year or so later, Billstarted building and preparing to open his second movie housein rural South Carolina. In the early 1930s there were no interstates, so going back and forth from Charlotte to South Carolina took time.

Bill was managing and running his first movie house in Charlotte, which meant he didn't have much time to go back and forth, so he decided to hire his first manager. He didn't know many people in that town, but he knew he could not be driving back and forth every day, especially since he also had a young wife who was working in a textile factory, and they were expecting their first child. Bill went to his mentor and asked him for advice on how he should make his first big hire.

Bill's mentor told him that this would probably be the most critical hire he would make. Bill needed to speak to a few people before he hired someone. His mentor told him that when the best and most successful owners need to make an essential hire, instinct is usually better than investigation.

Bill told me he didn't have a lot of time to find out about his candidates and went with his gut, his instinct. He ended up hiring a person who stayed with him through the years, through good times and bad times. That manager grew with Bill and ultimately became a partner with him on some other properties and restaurants. Bill told me that when hiring someone for a crucial position, yes, if you have time to do an investigation, do it, but your instinct usually turns out better than all the analysis.

I followed that advice when I was hiring hotel and restaurant managers and throughout my career, especially when I was adding people to the Tony Robbins security team. I go with my instinct first.

So, I told my young friend the answer to her question was that Bill used his instinct when he tossed me the keys to his Corvette and spent the ten minutes with me during the drive up and back on Woodlawn Road in Charlotte, North Carolina. His gut told him I was the one.

He had known me for seven months and had learned from our talks and from what I shared, and he knew that there was something special between us, and I would be open and coachable. After Bill passed away in 1997, Tony took me on to mentor me. He shared the reason he asked me to be his security director with me one day during our traditional walks before an event, and he later validated it on the evening of the Miracle on the Hudson.

Success does leave clues. Moments do matter. You never know which one of the moments in your life, at a specific time, will change the course of your life. Immerse yourself in these strategies and lessons to have personal success and fulfillment by applying the principles and habits. No single one may carry you to the pinnacle, but it will change your date with destiny.

Thank you for reading *From Turmoil to Triumph*.

Dave Sanderson

About the Author

Dave Sanderson

Dave Sanderson is the president of Dave Sanderson Speaks International based in Charlotte, North Carolina. On January 15, 2009, Dave was one of the last passengers off the plane that crashed into the Hudson River, best known as the Miracle on the Hudson, considered to be the most successful ditching in aviation history. He has built a career as a motivational speaker, mentor, and author and was recently named one of the Top 100 Leadership Speakers by Inc.com. Dave averages over eighty speeches a year for major corporations across the world.

In his presentations, he uses his experiences of being a top sales producer, serving as director of security for Tony Robbins, and surviving the plane crash to inspire and teach others. Dave explains how, through employing the personal leadership skills you have, you can find your distinct advantage in life and discover how you can use that to have not only a successful and fruitful life, but more importantly, a fulfilling life focused on serving others first.

Dave has spoken at countless fundraisers to help raise over $14 million for the American Red Cross. He continues to donate his speaking services to the organization as an expression of gratitude for the care he received from the first person he saw after he was rescued and transferred to land in New Jersey: a Red Cross volunteer with a blanket.

His book, *Moments Matter*, details the lessons learned from the Miracle on the Hudson and how one defining moment can create a lifetime of purpose so you can create your own "flight plan" for your future.

Dave hosts a Daily Flash Briefing, Voice of Personal Leadership, on the Alexa platform on Amazon every weekday, sharing lessons and strategies he employs for personal leadership so others can be inspired to utilize their personal leadership skills to become the servant leaders they are meant to be.

In his TEDx Talk, "Bouncing Back: An Experience with Post-Traumatic Growth Syndrome," Dave shares strategies on how to grow from your own "personal plane crash" to thriving. This is part of a new area of research on post-traumatic growth syndrome (PTGS), recently profiled in AARP.

Dave has been a faculty member with Dominique Wilkins, Don Barden, Brittany Tucker, and Steve Nedvidek at the Leadership Mindset Series based in Atlanta, Georgia. Dave knows a true leader understands that support from others can provide the tools needed to be an even stronger role model.

In his exclusive group, The Voice of Personal Leadership, Dave helps his team grow in their leadership skills. With proximity to like-minded, focused servant leaders, his team learns to impact the emotions, finances, spiritual lives, physical lives, and relationships of others.

Dave has recently rolled out an online course, Cultivating Personal Leadership, in which he shares the best strategies he has learned from some of the greatest leaders he studied under and met personally. He has implemented their methods in his life to become a top producer, sought-after speaker, author, and entrepreneur.

With a BBA in international business, Dave began his professional career in restaurant management. He went on to work as a national sales manager for ADP, management consultant for KPMG, senior vice president of sales for Genesis10, sales manager for Oracle, and security director for Robbins Research International, Inc., an Anthony Robbins Company.

He lives in Charlotte, North Carolina, with his wife, Terri, and their four children—Chelsey, Colleen, Courtney, and Chance.

Made in the USA
Monee, IL
13 October 2023

44516408R00144